STUDY GUIDE

No Other Gospel

Paul's Letter to the Galatians

Derek W.H. Thomas

LIGONIER MINISTRIES

Renew your Mind.

LIGONIER.ORG | 800-435-4343

Copyright © 2019 Ligonier Ministries
421 Ligonier Court, Sanford, FL 32771
E-mail: info@ligonier.org
All rights reserved.
No reproduction of this work without permission.
Printed in the United States of America.

Contents

Introduction

Christians must hold fast to the truth of the gospel. When false teachers were distorting the gospel among the churches in Galatia, the Apostle Paul wrote an impassioned letter in order to defend the message of God's grace in Christ. In *No Other Gospel*, Dr. Thomas walks us through the background, teaching, and importance of the letter to the Galatians. He encourages Christians to stand firm and rest in Christ for their salvation.

This study guide is a companion to the video teaching series. Whether you are using the DVDs, streaming the videos on Ligonier.org, or going through the course in Ligonier Connect, this resource is designed to help you make the most of the learning experience. For each message in the series, there is a corresponding lesson in this guide. Here is what you will find in each lesson:

INTRODUCTION	The introduction is a brief paragraph that summarizes the content covered in the lecture and considered in the study guide lesson.
	How to use: Use the introduction to each lesson to get a sense of the big picture before watching the video. Refer to these statements as you work through the study guide to remind you of what you have already covered and where you are headed.
LEARNING GOALS	The learning goals are the knowledge and skills that the study guide lesson will endeavor to equip you with as you work through the lecture content.
	How to use: Familiarize yourself with the goals of each lesson before engaging with its contents. Keeping the overall purpose in mind as you watch each video and reflect on or discuss the questions will help you get the most out of each lesson.
KEY IDEAS	The key ideas are the major points or takeaways from the lecture.
	How to use: Use these ideas to prepare yourself for each lesson and to review previous lessons. They describe specifically the knowledge that each lecture is communicating.

REFLECTION & DISCUSSION QUESTIONS	The questions are the guided reflection and/or discussion component of the lesson that is intended to help you prepare for, process, and organize what you are learning.
	How to use: Reflect on individually or discuss in a group the questions in the order in which they appear in the lesson. The time stamps in the right margin indicate where the answers to questions during the video can be found.
PRAYER	The prayer section offers suggestions for how to close the lesson in prayer with respect to what was taught in the lecture.
	How to use: Consider using each lesson's prayer section as a guide to personal or group prayer. These sections follow the ACTS prayer model, which you can learn more about in R.C. Sproul's Crucial Questions booklet *Does Prayer Change Things?* This helpful guide is available as a free e-book at Ligonier.org.
REVIEW QUIZ	The review quiz is a set of six multiple-choice questions that appears at the end of each lesson.
	How to use: Use each quiz to check your comprehension and memory of the major points covered in each lecture. It will be most beneficial to your learning if you take a lesson's quiz either sometime between lessons or just before you begin the next lesson in the study guide.
ANSWER KEY	The answer key provides explanations for the reflection and discussion questions and answers to the multiple-choice questions in the review quiz.
	How to use: Use the answer key to check your own answers or when you do not know the answer. Note: Do not give in too quickly; struggling for a few moments to recall an answer reinforces it in your mind.

Study Schedules

The following table suggests four plans for working through the *No Other Gospel* video teaching series and this companion study guide. Whether you are going through this series on your own or with a group, these schedules should help you plan your study path.

Week	Extended 16-Week Plan	Standard 14-Week Plan	Abbreviated 7-Week Plan	Intensive 4-Week Plan
	Lesson			
1	*	1	1 & 2	1–4
2	1	2	3 & 4	5–7
3	2	3	5 & 6	8–10
4	3	4	7 & 8	11–14
5	4	5	9 & 10	
6	5	6	11 & 12	
7	6	7	13 & 14	
8	7	8		
9	8	9		
10	9	10		
11	10	11		
12	11	12		
13	12	13		
14	13	14		
15	14			
16	*			

* For these weeks, rather than completing lessons, spend your time discussing and praying about your learning goals for the study (the first week) and the most valuable takeaways from the study (the last week).

1

The Only Gospel

INTRODUCTION

The grace of God in the gospel is central to the Christian faith. No sooner had the message of the gospel taken root in the churches of Galatia than false teachers began to disseminate a false gospel among new believers. In response, the Apostle Paul zealously defended the truth of the gospel for the preservation of Christianity. In this lesson, Dr. Thomas introduces us to the background and key factors involved in the Galatian controversy, along with the Apostle Paul's zeal to defend the gospel.

LEARNING GOALS

When you have finished this lesson, you should be able to:

- Define the gospel in accordance with the definition that the Apostle Paul gives in Galatians 1
- Identify the essence of the doctrinal error that Paul is addressing in this letter
- Understand why false gospels are destructive and why we must oppose them

KEY IDEAS

- The gospel is the proclamation of what Jesus has done on the cross to atone for the sin of His people and deliver them from the present evil age.
- The gospel was in jeopardy in the churches of Galatia because of a false gospel that the Judaizers were propagating.
- The Judaizers taught that gentile converts needed to believe in Jesus and keep the ceremonial law of Moses in order to be justified before God.
- The Apostle Paul pronounced the strongest possible imprecation on the false teachers who were spreading a false gospel among believers.

REFLECTION & DISCUSSION QUESTIONS

Before the Video

What Do You Think?

> Take a moment to answer the following questions. They will prepare you for the lecture.
>
> - Why are you interested in undertaking this study of the book of Galatians?
>
> - How familiar are you with the doctrine of justification? Can you define it? What impact does the doctrine of justification have on your daily relationship with God?

Scripture Reading

> *I am astonished that you are so quickly deserting him who called you in the grace of Christ and are turning to a different gospel—not that there is another one, but there are some who trouble you and want to distort the gospel of Christ. But even if we or an angel from heaven should preach to you a gospel contrary to the one we preached to you, let him be accursed.*
>
> —Galatians 1:6–8
>
> - What does this passage reveal about the degree to which we should be committed to defending the purity of the gospel?

During the Video

> Answer the following questions while you watch the video. They will guide you through the lecture.

Defining the Gospel *0:00–11:00*

> - What significant role did the book of Galatians play in the Reformation?
>
> - What is the heart of the message of Galatians?
>
> - How does Dr. Thomas define the gospel in this lesson?

Distorting the Gospel   *11:00–18:03*

- Who were the Judaizers? What was the essence of the false gospel that they were propagating among the members of the churches of Galatia?

- What important qualification did the Apostle Paul make after expressing surprise that many professing believers were turning to another gospel?

Discerning the Gospel   *18:03–23:12*

- What pronouncement did Paul make against those who preach a false gospel?

- What conclusion were the members of the church to come to about the nature of the Judaizers in order to stand against their false teaching?

After the Video

Answer the following questions after you have finished the lecture. They will help you identify and summarize the major points.

- Which person of the Godhead initiated the plan of salvation?

  If you are in a group, have the members discuss how they tend to view the role that God the Father plays in the work of redemption. Consider asking questions such as these: Why do you believe that we have a tendency to think about the Son as the One who makes the Father willing to be gracious to us? How does a right understanding of the Father's role in initiating the plan of salvation magnify the grace of the gospel?

- Why is the insistence that one has to observe the Jewish law in order to be right with God destructive of the true gospel?

  If you are in a group, have the members discuss the various ways that we may subtly fall into the trap of adding something to the finished work of Christ for a right standing with God. Consider questions such as this: Do you ever think or act as though your standing with God were based on something other than or in addition to Christ?

• How can believers be zealous to maintain the truth of the gospel?

If you are in a group, have each member discuss the importance of preaching the gospel to himself or herself. Consider asking questions such as these: How often do you purposefully preach the gospel to yourself? What practical benefit is there to preaching the gospel to yourself?

PRAYER

Commit what you have learned from God's Word in this lesson to prayer.

• Praise God for revealing the truth of the gospel of God's grace in Christ to you.
• Confess the ways in which you have acted as though your acceptance with God were based on your attempts to keep His law.
• Thank God for the perfect work of Jesus Christ in atoning for your sins and providing you with a perfect righteousness.
• Ask God to help you see your continual need for the gospel.

REVIEW QUIZ

Use these multiple-choice questions to measure what you learned from this lesson.

1. Which theologian wrote a commentary on Galatians that fueled the Reformation?
   a. John Calvin
   b. John Bunyan
   c. Martin Luther
   d. Martin Bucer

2. What problem does the gospel primarily deal with?
   a. Our unhappiness
   b. Our discontentment
   c. Our sense of acceptance
   d. Our sin

3. To what does the phrase "the present evil age" refer?
   a. The first-century world under Roman rule
   b. This fallen world in contrast with the world to come
   c. The Judaizing culture in Jerusalem
   d. The twenty-first-century world

4. What did the Judaizers say that gentile converts needed to do to be justified?
   a. Observe the moral law of Moses
   b. Observe the ceremonial law of Moses
   c. Observe the civil law of Moses
   d. Observe the entire Mosaic law

5. What phrase did Dr. Thomas use to summarize the Judaizers' false gospel?
    a. "A matter of second principles"
    b. "A damnable plus"
    c. "The circumcision party"
    d. "Moralistic therapeutic deism"

6. What does the word *anathematize* mean?
    a. "To accurse"
    b. "To publicly denounce"
    c. "To debate"
    d. "To reconcile"

Answer Key—The Only Gospel

REFLECTION & DISCUSSION QUESTIONS

Before the Video

What Do You Think?

These are personal questions. The answers should be based on your own knowledge and experience.

Scripture Reading

- What does this passage reveal about the degree to which we should be committed to defending the purity of the gospel?

  The surprise expressed by the Apostle gives us a sense of the degree to which we should be concerned about the purity of the gospel. Paul uses the strongest possible language in order to defend the gospel in the letter to the Galatians. He writes this letter to repudiate any attempt to substitute the true gospel with a false gospel and calls the members of the church to be discerning whenever someone comes to them with a substitute for the gospel that they had received from him.

During the Video

Defining the Gospel

- What significant role did the book of Galatians play in the Reformation?

  Paul's letter to the Galatians played a significant role in the Reformation because Martin Luther wrote a highly significant commentary on it. Luther's commentary helped set the Reformation on the trajectory of defending the doctrine of justification against the Roman Catholic perversion of it.

- What is the heart of the message of Galatians?

  At the heart of the message of Galatians is the question, What is the gospel? Justification by faith alone in Christ alone apart from the works of the law is the essence of the gospel. Paul's zeal reflected his commitment to the defense of the core gospel message.

- How does Dr. Thomas define the gospel in this lesson?

  In this lesson, Dr. Thomas defined the gospel as "a message of grace." It is the message of "the giving of Jesus for our sins to deliver us from this present evil age, and all this is part of the sovereign will of our heavenly Father; it's a message of grace." Since sin is our great problem, the gospel is the message about how God has dealt with our sin through the death and resurrection of Jesus.

Distorting the Gospel

- Who were the Judaizers? What was the essence of the false gospel that they were propagating among the members of the church of Galatia?

  The Judaizers were teaching the members of the churches in Galatia that they needed to trust in Christ and keep the law of Moses in order to be justified before God. They were concerned about the place of the gentiles in the church. They insisted that in order to be real Christians, gentiles needed to observe the Jewish ceremonial laws. These false teachers were concerned that gentile converts weren't circumcised, didn't observe Jewish food laws, and didn't observe the ceremonial calendar, such as the feasts of Passover and Tabernacles. These were the ceremonial boundary markers that set Jews apart from gentiles. The Judaizers were seeking to impose these Old Testament provisional laws on the gentiles.

- What important qualification did the Apostle Paul make after expressing surprise that many professing believers were turning to another gospel?

  Immediately after expressing his shock that many in the church were turning away from the true gospel to another gospel, Paul explained that there is not actually another gospel. There is only one true gospel. There are not multiple gospels. The true gospel saves; all alternative messages lead to condemnation. There can be no substitute for the one message of salvation by grace alone through faith alone in Christ alone.

Discerning the Gospel

- What pronouncement did Paul make against those who preach a false gospel?

  The Apostle used the strongest possible language to denounce the false gospel that the Judaizers were propagating. He said that if anyone is preaching another gospel, he should be "accursed" (Gal. 1:8–9). The meaning of the word "accursed" here is "anathematized"—which means "driven away from the grace and presence of God." Paul included even the Apostles and angels from heaven among those regarding whom the members of the church were to exercise discernment.

- What conclusion were the members of the church to come to about the nature of the Judaizers in order to stand against their false teaching?

  The members of the church in Galatia were to recognize that the Judaizers were wolves in sheep's clothing. As those who had embraced the true gospel, they were to view the Judaizers for what they were in reality—wolves. Paul was calling believers to acknowledge that these wolves were in the church and in fellowship with them.

After the Video

- Which person of the Godhead initiated the plan of salvation?

  In the lesson, Dr. Thomas made the important point that the Father takes the initiative in the plan of salvation. As the Apostle John explains in John 3:16, it is

God the Father who gave His only begotten Son. The Son of God did not make a reluctant Father willing to be gracious to us. We often mistakenly think that God the Father will have mercy on us because of Christ, when in reality the mercy and love of the Father are demonstrated in His giving His Son for us.

- Why is the insistence that one has to observe the Jewish law in order to be right with God destructive of the true gospel?

Adding anything to the finished work of Christ undermines the truth that salvation is through Christ alone. Insisting that the gospel is Jesus plus anything is, in the words of Dr. Thomas, "a damnable plus for Paul." It is no longer good news if we add anything to Jesus for our justification. The gospel that Paul preached is the same as the message of the solas of the Reformation. It is a message of salvation by faith alone in Christ alone apart from works of the law.

- How can believers be zealous to maintain the truth of the gospel?

We first have to know the true gospel. Once we have come to know and believe the gospel, we have to preach the message of the gospel to ourselves every day. We can never meditate on the gospel too much. Every morning, we should call to mind the message of the gospel.

REVIEW QUIZ

Lesson 1

1. **C.**

Martin Luther wrote a commentary on Paul's letter to the Galatians that became extremely influential in the Reformation. In this work, Luther sets out his own experience of coming to a biblical understanding of the doctrine of justification by faith alone. This book continued to influence Reformed theologians after the Reformation too. For instance, in his autobiography, John Bunyan noted the significant role that Luther's commentary had played in his own spiritual development.

2. **D.**

The gospel primarily deals with our problem of sin. The death and resurrection of Jesus does not, first and foremost, deal with our desire for happiness, contentment, or acceptance. Paul defines the central message of the gospel when he says that Jesus "gave himself for our sins" (Gal. 1:4). Jesus' death was an atonement for sin—a substitutionary sacrifice to deal with our sin.

3. **B.**

When Paul speaks of Jesus' delivering us from "the present evil age," he has this fallen world—under the sway of the evil one—in view. He was drawing a contrast between this present fallen age and the world to come. The Apostle is anticipating the renewal of all things in the new heavens and new earth in which righteousness will dwell. Christ has died to secure for His people the future hope of the world to come.

4. **B.**

   The Judaizers were wrongfully binding the consciences of gentile believers by insisting that they needed to keep the ceremonial law (i.e., food laws, ceremonial festivals, and circumcision) for their justification. These things had been given by God to Israel in the Old Testament and were no longer binding once Christ came and fulfilled the purpose of these ceremonial laws.

5. **B.**

   Dr. Thomas used the phrase "a damnable plus" to explain the way in which the Apostle Paul viewed the essence of the false teaching of the Judaizers. They were telling the members of the church that they needed Jesus and also needed to observe circumcision, dietary laws, and the Jewish festival calendar in order to be justified. Anything we add to Jesus for a right standing before God is classified as "a damnable plus." Adding anything to Jesus for our justification is a denial of solus Christus—*Christ alone.*

6. **A.**

   The word anathematize *means "to accurse." It is the strongest possible denunciation that the Apostle Paul could have pronounced on those who propagate a false gospel. With this pronouncement, Paul was expressing his desire to see anyone who promotes a counterfeit gospel driven far away from the grace, love, and embrace of God.*

2

The Apostle's Defense

INTRODUCTION

In the introduction of his letter to the Galatians, the Apostle Paul offered a definition of the gospel along with a warning about the destructive nature of false gospels. Because certain false teachers were attacking the legitimacy of Paul's ministry in an attempt to undermine the gospel, Paul needed to defend his own ministry and Apostleship. In this lesson, Dr. Thomas focuses our attention on the significance of Paul's teaching about his past, his conversion, and the origin of his gospel.

LEARNING GOALS

When you have finished this lesson, you should be able to:

- Identify the specific ways in which the members of the churches in Galatia were attacking the legitimacy of Paul's ministry
- Explain the various steps Paul took to defend his ministry against those who attacked him

KEY IDEAS

- Paul appealed to his history of violently persecuting the church before his conversion to defend his reputation for the sake of his present ministry.
- The eternal, sovereign purpose of God in Paul's conversion was an essential part of Paul's defense against the unjust attacks launched against him in Galatia.
- To justify the legitimacy of his ministry, Paul defended the divine origin of his gospel message.

REFLECTION & DISCUSSION QUESTIONS

Before the Video

What Do You Think?

Take a moment to answer the following questions. They will prepare you for the lecture.

- How does Paul's conversion affect our understanding of the gospel?

- Why is it important to identify the origins of the gospel?

Scripture Reading

For I would have you know, brothers, that the gospel that was preached by me is not man's gospel. For I did not receive it from any man, nor was I taught it, but I received it through a revelation of Jesus Christ.

—Galatians 1:11–12

- Why did the Apostle Paul defend the origin of the gospel he preached?

During the Video

Answer the following questions while you watch the video. They will guide you through the lecture.

Paul's Past   *0:00–8:39*

- Why did Paul appeal to his past in this passage?

- How did Paul defend his ministry against the unjust attacks he was enduring?

Paul's Conversion   *8:39–16:55*

- In what unusual way did Paul speak about his conversion?

- What special phrase did Paul use to describe his conversion?

Paul's Gospel   *16:55–23:47*

- What special privilege did the other Apostles have that Paul did not have? What gave them an advantage over him in this respect?

- If Paul didn't learn the gospel from men, how did he learn it?

After the Video

Answer the following questions after you have finished the lecture. They will help you identify and summarize the major points.

- How did Paul classify his former religious convictions?

If you are in a group, have the members discuss the ways in which we can wrongly be zealous for something while believing that we are serving God.

- How did Paul speak about the way in which God revealed Christ to him?

If you are in a group, have the members discuss the importance of having Christ dwell in our hearts. Consider asking questions such as these: Do you ever pray that you would know more of the indwelling of Christ in your heart? How does Christ dwell in us?

- Why was Peter such an important figure in the early church?

If you are in a group, have the members discuss what we can learn about the grace of God from the life of Peter. In what ways does Peter's life teach us that God uses weak and broken people to build His church?

PRAYER

Commit what you have learned from God's Word in this lesson to prayer.

- Praise God for calling and transforming you by His grace.
- Confess ways in which you have failed to be zealous in the defense of the gospel.
- Thank God for opening your eyes to believe in the divine origin of the gospel.
- Ask God for more opportunities to share the gospel with others so that Christ might be formed in them.

REVIEW QUIZ

Use these multiple-choice questions to measure what you learned from this lesson.

1. In the book of Acts, why does the Apostle have two names, Saul of Tarsus and Paul?
    a. Saul was his name before conversion; Paul was his name after conversion.
    b. Paul was his Hebrew name; Saul was his Greek name.
    c. Saul was his Hebrew name; Paul was his Greek name.
    d. Saul is to Abram as Paul is to Abraham.

2. What word did Dr. Thomas use to describe Paul's past?
    a. Conservative
    b. Progressive
    c. Violent
    d. Indifferent

3. In what way did Paul speak about God's revelation of Christ to him?
    a. "He was pleased to reveal his Son to me."
    b. "He was pleased to reveal his Son to me in Scripture."
    c. "He was pleased to reveal his Son through the preaching of the Apostles."
    d. "He was pleased to reveal his Son to me through a vision."

4. What divine title did James use when speaking of Jesus?
    a. Savior
    b. Lord
    c. God
    d. Judge

5. Where did Paul go immediately after he was converted?
    a. Jerusalem
    b. Galatia
    c. Damascus
    d. Arabia

6. To whom did the Holy Spirit send Paul for affirmation of the gospel that he had received directly from Christ?
    a. Peter
    b. James
    c. John
    d. All of the above

Answer Key—The Apostle's Defense

Before the Video

What Do You Think?

> These are personal questions. The answers should be based on your own knowledge and experience.

Scripture Reading

- Why did the Apostle Paul defend the origin of the gospel he preached?

    The Judaizers were attacking Paul to undermine the message of the gospel that Paul was defending in Galatia. In response, the Apostle indicated that the divine origin of the gospel gave it an authority that the false teachers lacked. It was not a man-made gospel. Paul had not received it from men; he had received it directly from Jesus Christ.

During the Video

Paul's Past

- Why did Paul appeal to his past in this passage?

    The Judaizers were accusing Paul of being an impostor and a newcomer. They may have been implying that Paul had cast off his love for the Jewish people and for the Jewish tradition of which he had formerly been a part. Since the Judaizers insisted on the observance of the ceremonial law, they were likely suggesting that Paul had become a theological liberal. Paul explained that he had not become less conservative, but rather that God had revealed to him the right understanding of the gospel.

- How did Paul defend his ministry against the unjust attacks he was enduring?

    Paul told the members of the churches in Galatia, "You have heard of my former life in Judaism, how I persecuted the church of God violently and tried to destroy it" (Gal. 1:13). In this way, he was weakening their present attacks by reminding them that there was no new information about him. They already knew who he had been and who God had made him by grace. Paul had been zealous for the Jewish faith and a persecutor of the Christian church before his conversion. Paul reminded the members of the church of this fact to show that he had been converted by the grace of God in Christ and had been awakened to the truth of the gospel.

Paul's Conversion

- In what unusual way did Paul speak about his conversion?

  Rather than referring to the Damascus road experience—during which Paul was confronted and converted by the risen Jesus—he spoke of being set apart by God before he was born (Gal. 1:15). Paul was intimating that his conversion was rooted in God's eternal plan. He was making a statement about the sovereignty of God in speaking of his conversion in this way.

- What special phrase did Paul use to describe his conversion?

  In Galatians 1:15, Paul referred to God as He "who called me by his grace." Paul understood that the new birth he had experienced was nothing less than an effectual divine calling. Paul uses the same wording in 1 Corinthians when he speaks of the regeneration of believers. He addressed the believers in Corinth as those who had been "called to be saints" or "holy called ones" (1:2).

Paul's Gospel

- What special privilege did the other Apostles have that Paul did not have? What gave them an advantage over him in this respect?

  The other Apostles had been with Jesus during His earthly ministry. They had seen His miracles. They had heard His preaching and teaching. They could bear witness to the fact that they had seen and heard all that Jesus did and said. They could verify that they had been together as they witnessed Jesus' messianic ministry. Paul could not do the same. He didn't have the same sort of firsthand knowledge of the earthly ministry of Christ. Though he had personally met the risen Jesus on the Damascus road, Paul couldn't speak of His earthly ministry in the way that the other Apostles could.

- If Paul didn't learn the gospel from men, how did he learn it?

  In Galatians 1:12, Paul explained that he had not received the gospel from men. Rather, he had been taught it directly by a revelation of Jesus Christ. He then defended this truth by bearing witness to the fact that after he was converted, he did not immediately meet with the other Apostles. Rather, he went to Arabia. In Arabia, Paul read the Scriptures, diligently studied them, and received revelations, insight, knowledge, and understanding directly from the Holy Spirit.

After the Video

- How did Paul classify his former religious convictions?

  In Galatians 1:13, Paul spoke of his former religious convictions as "my former life in Judaism." This was an intentional way of distancing himself from Judaism. Paul had not been a religious conservative and then become a religious progressive. Rather, he had been converted out of the very thing to which the Judaizers were seeking to seduce the Christian converts in Galatia. Paul explained that his former life in Judaism was one in which he had severely persecuted the church.

- How did Paul speak about the way in which God revealed Christ to him?

In Galatians 1:16, Paul said that God "was pleased to reveal his Son to me." Some English translations have a footnote in which the translators explain that the words translated "to me" can also be translated "in me." If we adopt this latter reading, the idea is that Jesus was not just revealed to Paul; He was sent by God the Father to dwell in Paul's heart. Paul was a Christian because Jesus was revealed in him.

- Why was Peter such an important figure in the early church?

In addition to having personally been with Jesus throughout the entirety of His earthly ministry, Peter was the chief among equals in the Apostolic band. Peter was the one to whom Jesus said, "You are Peter, and on this rock I will build my church, and the gates of hell shall not prevail against it" (Matt. 16:18). Peter was the central figure in the first twelve chapters of the book of Acts. Despite Peter's denial of the Lord, Jesus chose to use him to be the foremost Apostle and the great preacher on the day of Pentecost.

REVIEW QUIZ

Lesson 2

1. **C.**

   Some suggest that the name Paul was the name that God gave Saul of Tarsus when He saved him on the Damascus road. However, it is more likely that the Apostle always had two names, one Hebrew and the other Greek. Saul was the Apostle's Hebrew name, and Paul was his Greek name. When he ministered in Hellenistic cities like Galatia, he would have used his Greek name, Paul, for the sake of the spread of the gospel.

2. **C.**

   Dr. Thomas described Paul's past as violent. Saul of Tarsus tried to destroy the Christian church before his conversion. He wrote letters that enabled other Jews to arrest Christian men, women, and children. He may have even had some of the early Christians killed for their faith in Christ. He consented to the death of Stephen, the first Christian martyr.

3. **A.**

   Paul explained the way in which God had revealed Christ to him by saying, "He . . . was pleased to reveal his Son to me" (Gal. 1:15–16). The revelation of Christ to Paul wasn't simply an objective revelation of the truth about the Son of God; it was a subjective revelation of Christ to convert and convince Paul. Jesus came to indwell Paul. He opened Paul's heart to see the truth of the gospel.

4. **B.**

James, Jesus' earthly brother, called Jesus "Lord" in his epistle. This was a recognition of the deity of Christ. James didn't view Jesus according to his human relationship with Him as a brother. Rather, he worshiped Him and ascribed to Him the title Lord.

5. **D.**

Immediately after his conversion, Paul went to Arabia. He did not go up to Jerusalem to see the Apostles first. This is an important detail in the defense of his ministry because it was in Arabia that the Lord taught Paul and instructed him in the gospel. Paul would have studied Scripture there and may have experienced direct visions from the Lord. This substantiates his claim that he was not taught the gospel from men. Only after he had spent several years in Arabia did the Apostle Paul go up to the other Apostles.

6. **D.**

The Holy Spirit directed Paul to go up and meet with Peter, James, and John in order to communicate the gospel he had received from the Lord. At that time, Paul spent fifteen days with Peter discussing what had happened to him and the details of the gospel. This proves that the gospel Paul preached did not come from Peter. Paul was not an impostor, seeking to imitate the other Apostles. He was not preaching a man's gospel. It was the gospel from God.

3

Threats to the Gospel

INTRODUCTION

In Galatians 1, the Apostle Paul defends his ministry from the attacks of those who crept into the church to promote a false gospel. In this lesson, Dr. Thomas reflects on Paul's move to defend the gospel by exposing the nature of the threat that a false gospel poses to our freedom in Christ in Galatians 2.

LEARNING GOALS

When you have finished this lesson, you should be able to:

- Recognize the specific threat to the gospel in Galatians 2
- Explain the historical situation that Paul was reacting against
- Identify the key figures involved in the controversy in Jerusalem over circumcision

KEY IDEAS

- The book of Galatians is about defending the spiritual freedom that we have in Christ.
- By insisting that circumcision was necessary for justification, Jewish false teachers were circulating a false gospel among the church.
- Paul stood for the truth of the gospel against the opinions and influence of others.
- Peter, James, and John acknowledged the call of God on the Apostle Paul, thereby affirming the gospel he preached.

REFLECTION & DISCUSSION QUESTIONS

Before the Video

What Do You Think?

Take a moment to answer the following questions. They will prepare you for the lecture.

- In what ways can we compromise the truth of the gospel?

- How should we view the old covenant ceremonial laws, such as circumcision, dietary laws, and annual feasts?

Scripture Reading

Then after fourteen years I went up again to Jerusalem with Barnabas, taking Titus along with me. I went up because of a revelation and set before them (though privately before those who seemed influential) the gospel that I proclaim among the Gentiles, in order to make sure I was not running or had not run in vain. But even Titus, who was with me, was not forced to be circumcised, though he was a Greek. Yet because of false brothers secretly brought in—who slipped in to spy out our freedom that we have in Christ Jesus, so that they might bring us into slavery—to them we did not yield in submission even for a moment, so that the truth of the gospel might be preserved for you.

—Galatians 2:1–5

- What does this passage teach us about the Apostle Paul's commitment to defending the gospel?

During the Video

Answer the following questions while you watch the video. They will guide you through the lecture.

Gospel Threat   *0:00–15:00*

- To which past controversy did Paul appeal in his defense of the gospel against the attacks of the Judaizers?

- Why did Paul formerly consent to Timothy's circumcision while adamantly insisting that Titus not be circumcised in Jerusalem?

- How was the matter of Titus' circumcision a racial issue?

Gospel Triumph   15:00–22:58

- How did Peter, James, and John respond when Paul came to meet them in Jerusalem in order to present his gospel before them?

- What did the reception of Paul by the other Apostles indicate in regard to the present controversy?

- After they agreed on the gospel, what was the thing that all the Apostles agreed should be done?

After the Video

Answer the following questions after you have finished the lecture. They will help you identify and summarize the major points.

- What single word can we use to describe the central message of the letter to the Galatians?

  If you are in a group, have the members discuss spiritual freedom. What does it mean that we are free in Christ? What misconception might we have about spiritual freedom? How do we preserve freedom in our churches?

- According to Dr. Thomas, what are some of the ways that we can jeopardize the gospel with our insistence on things that are not the gospel?

  If you are in a group, have the members discuss the various ways in which we often want to add our preferences to the gospel. Consider asking questions such as this: If someone doesn't share your particular conviction on something that is not central to the gospel, how do you tend to respond?

- What was Paul's response to the influential Apostles with whom he met about the issue with Titus? What was his disposition toward them?

  If you are in a group, have the members discuss how easy it is to be swayed by the opinions and influence of others. Consider asking questions such as this: How difficult do you think it was for Paul to take a stand by himself when he was in the presence of respected Apostles?

PRAYER

Commit what you have learned from God's Word in this lesson to prayer.

• Praise God for the freedom that you have experienced in Christ.
• Confess the times you have made personal preferences or secondary matters central to the gospel.
• Thank God for enabling you to understand the truth of justification by faith alone.
• Ask God to keep you grounded in the truth of the gospel.

REVIEW QUIZ

Use these multiple-choice questions to measure what you learned from this lesson.

1. Where did Paul go by revelation in order to set his gospel before the leading Apostles?
   a. Arabia
   b. Galatia
   c. Antioch
   d. Jerusalem

2. Who were the three most important disciples of Christ?
   a. Peter, James, and Paul
   b. Paul, James, and John
   c. Peter, James, and John
   d. None of the above

3. Whom did Paul take with him to Jerusalem when he went to meet with the other Apostles?
   a. Timothy
   b. Titus
   c. John Mark
   d. Apollos

4. To which group was Peter commissioned by God to preach the gospel?
   a. To those in Antioch
   b. To those in Galatia
   c. To the Jews
   d. To the gentiles

5. When Paul went up to Jerusalem to meet with Peter, James, and John, he insisted on discussing the matter of the gospel publicly.
   a. True
   b. False

6. Whom did the Apostles have in mind when they spoke of remembering "the poor"?
    a. The poor in spirit
    b. The poor in Galatia
    c. The poor Jewish Christians
    d. The poor gentiles in Antioch

Answer Key—Threats to the Gospel

REFLECTION & DISCUSSION QUESTIONS

Before the Video

What Do You Think?

> *These are personal questions. The answers should be based on your own knowledge and experience.*

Scripture Reading

- What does this passage teach us about the Apostle Paul's commitment to defending the gospel?

  Paul explains that he did not "yield in submission even for a moment" to false brothers who came into the church to enslave members by insisting that they adhere to the ceremonial law of Moses for justification.

During the Video

Gospel Threat

- To which past controversy did Paul appeal in his defense of the gospel against the attacks of the Judaizers?

  The Apostle told the members of the church in Galatia about a related incident that had occurred after his first visit with Peter in Jerusalem. In this instance, Paul had taken Titus with him. Titus was a gentile and therefore was not circumcised. This meant that to the Jews in Jerusalem, Titus was considered unclean. The Apostle Paul refused to have Titus circumcised despite the insistence of the Jewish people.

- Why did Paul formerly consent to Timothy's circumcision while adamantly insisting that Titus not be circumcised in Jerusalem?

  In the case of Timothy, the gospel was not in jeopardy. The Judaizers had connected Titus' circumcision to the gospel. They had essentially said, "Believe in Jesus—but you also need to be circumcised if you are going to be saved."

- How was the matter of Titus' circumcision a racial issue?

  Titus was a gentile and had never received the sign of circumcision. The Jews viewed him as unclean. By suggesting that he needed to be circumcised, they were—by implication—suggesting that he was not fully acceptable to God without it. While we often speak of anti-Semitic racism, the discrimination the Jews showed Titus was a form of racist anti-gentilism.

Gospel Triumph

- How did Peter, James, and John respond when Paul came to meet them in Jerusalem in order to present his gospel before them?

  Though the gospel and the unity of the Christian church was at stake, these three Apostles acknowledged that God had called them to take the gospel to the Jews and that He had called Paul, Barnabas, and Titus to take the same gospel to the gentiles. They received and welcomed Paul after their meeting with him.

- What did the reception of Paul by the other Apostles indicate in regard to the present controversy?

  The controversy surrounding the circumcision of Titus came to a conclusion with Peter, James, and John recognizing that God had appointed some of them to take the gospel to the Jews and some of them to take the gospel to the gentiles. In Galatians 2:9, we read, "When James and Cephas and John . . . perceived the grace that was given to me, they gave the right hand of fellowship to Barnabas and me, that we should go to the Gentiles and they to the circumcised." They were in agreement that they were to proclaim the same gospel to the different people groups.

- After they agreed on the gospel, what was the thing that all the Apostles agreed should be done?

  All the Apostles present in Jerusalem agreed that they should remember the poor. Jewish converts to Christianity commonly suffered ostracism from family and the business community. On account of this, poverty was a real problem for many Christians in Jerusalem. In order to address this problem, Peter, James, John, and Paul agreed that they should all be attentive to the needs of the poor believers in Jerusalem. This was the only requirement placed on the gentiles. There was no requirement to keep the Jewish ceremonial law or to have Titus circumcised.

After the Video

- What single word can we use to describe the central message of the letter to the Galatians?

  The book of Galatians is about freedom. *Christians are free from any obligation to keep the law for their justification. Believers are free from the burden of the law. This is central to the message of Galatians, particularly in chapters 5–6. The threat to the message of the gospel in Galatians was the same threat that Paul experienced in Jerusalem. In that case, false brothers had crept into the church to spy out the new converts' freedom. They wanted to bring them back into slavery of law-keeping for justification.*

- According to Dr. Thomas, what are some of the ways that we can jeopardize the gospel with our insistence on things that are not the gospel?

  Though we may not be likely to compromise the gospel by insisting on circumcision, we can easily fall into the snare of elevating other things that are not central to the gospel. For instance, we may insist that you are not a Christian unless you are committed to a particular translation of the Bible, or to homeschooling, or to a particular political party, or to a certain view on head coverings, or to a certain view on alcohol. Any of these things can become a damnable plus to the message of the gospel.

- What was Paul's response to the influential Apostles with whom he met about the issue with Titus? What was his disposition toward them?

  In Galatians 2:6, Paul called those with whom he went to meet "those who seemed to be influential." Though he was a younger man, Paul was not swayed by public opinion or seeming public influence. He said concerning them, "What they were makes no difference to me; God shows no partiality." Paul was not being belligerent in his response to Peter and those with him. Rather, he was not allowing himself to be swayed by the status of others.

REVIEW QUIZ

Lesson 3

1. **D.**

   Paul went up to Jerusalem because of a revelation from God in order to set his gospel before the leading Apostles. The location of this meeting is important because of the conflict that Paul would experience in Jerusalem over the issue of circumcision. In the early days of Christianity in Jerusalem, many Christians still worshiped in the synagogue. Many of the Jewish Christians still had a Jewish mind-set and were finding it difficult to understand the differences between the old and new covenants.

2. **C.**

   Peter, James, and John were the three leading Apostles. They had formed Jesus' inner circle during His earthly ministry. They had been with Him on the Mount of Transfiguration. They had seen Him raise a little girl from the dead. They were eyewitnesses of Jesus' glory. Jesus had set them apart, in a sense, for the foundation of the new covenant church. This made them the three most important disciples of Christ.

3. **B.**

   When Paul went up to Jerusalem to set his gospel before the Apostles, he took Titus with him. Titus was a Greek by birth and was therefore uncircumcised. Titus' presence in Jerusalem set the stage for the conflict over the Jews' insistence that he needed to be circumcised. Paul would not submit to their demands because he understood that they were jeopardizing the gospel with their insistence on circumcision.

4. **C.**

   The Lord called Peter to be the Apostle to the Jews. Paul explained the significance of this when he wrote, "I had been entrusted with the gospel to the uncircumcised, just as Peter had been entrusted with the gospel to the circumcised" (Gal. 2:7). There was only one gospel for Jew and gentile. Peter was called to preach the same gospel that Paul preached, but he was called to preach specifically to the Jewish people.

5. **B.**

   The Apostle Paul set his gospel before the leading Apostles in private. He didn't make a public show of the matter. He handled the matter discreetly. In this lesson, Dr. Thomas made an application from this that not everything needs to be made public. Christians need to learn that we don't need to publicize all our opinions on social media and other public platforms. When the gospel is at stake, it is sometimes better for the unity of the church that things be handled privately.

6. **C.**

   It was common for Jewish Christians in Jerusalem in the first century to experience social, familial, and commercial ostracism. This in turn led to their impoverishment. The Apostles agreed that while there was nothing about the Jewish ceremonial law that the gentiles needed to observe, the gentile believers ought to give special attention to caring for the poor Jewish Christians in Jerusalem.

4

Paul Opposes Peter

INTRODUCTION

After the Apostle Paul introduces his defense of the gospel in his letter to the Galatians, he recounts his interaction with the Apostle Peter in Antioch. Peter jeopardized the truth of the gospel by refusing to eat with gentile converts, and Paul opposed Peter for this to his face. In this lesson, Dr. Thomas expounds on the importance of Paul's confrontation with Peter.

LEARNING GOALS

When you have finished this lesson, you should be able to:

- Explain the context in which the conflict between Paul and Peter occurred in Antioch
- Describe how the Judaizers were denying justification by faith by insisting that the gentiles keep the ceremonial law
- Understand the various ways in which we too can deny justification by faith alone by adding obligations to what Christ had accomplished for us through His death

KEY IDEAS

- Peter sinfully withdrew and refused to eat nonkosher foods with gentile converts after he was pressured by certain men from Jerusalem.
- We can undermine the credibility of the beliefs we profess by our behavior.
- The Apostle teaches us the necessity of maintaining our identity in union with Christ.
- In the gospel, we have died to the demands and threats of the law in order that we might live to God.

REFLECTION & DISCUSSION QUESTIONS

Before the Video

What Do You Think?

Take a moment to answer the following questions. They will prepare you for the lecture.

- How does the gospel affect the way that we welcome believers of different ethnic or national backgrounds into the fellowship of our churches?

- Why can no one be justified by his or her attempts to obey the law?

Scripture Reading

We know that a person is not justified by works of the law but through faith in Jesus Christ, so we also have believed in Christ Jesus, in order to be justified by faith in Christ and not by works of the law, because by works of the law no one will be justified.

—Galatians 2:16

- How do the positive and negative statements in this passage reinforce the doctrine of justification by faith alone in Christ alone?

During the Video

Answer the following questions while you watch the video. They will guide you through the lecture.

Historical Narrative   *0:00–13:12*

- What brought about Peter's change of behavior toward gentile converts in Antioch?

- What were those from Jerusalem implying when they insisted that the gentile converts eat only kosher food?

Theological Reflection   *13:12–23:47*

- What role does obedience to the law play in our justification?

- What does Galatians 2:19 teach us about the relationship between our justification and a life of obedience?

After the Video

Answer the following questions after you have finished the lecture. They will help you identify and summarize the major points.

- What do we learn about the relationship between behavior and belief from Peter's actions?

  If you are in a group, have the members discuss various ways in which our behavior reflects what we believe. Consider asking questions such as these: If we are harsh and unmerciful to others in the church, what does that reveal about the way that we believe God deals with us? How about with regard to our interaction with unbelievers?

- Why is it vital for us to understand that union with Christ is the center of Paul's theology?

  If you are in a group, have the members discuss the way in which union with Christ affects our daily interactions with others and the assurance of our salvation. Consider asking questions such as this: How does union with Christ factor into our relationships with other believers in the church?

- What did Paul mean when he said that "through the law I died to the law"?

  If you are in a group, have the members discuss why it is so important for us to be reminded of this truth daily. Do you find that you are still terrified by the threats of the law? If so, what is the remedy?

PRAYER

Commit what you have learned from God's Word in this lesson to prayer.

- Praise God for making clear in His Word how all the ceremonial laws were fulfilled in Christ.
- Confess the ways in which you have denied what you have professed to believe about the gospel by your actions.
- Thank God for the unparalleled blessing of union with Christ.
- Ask God to enable you to walk in obedience through gratitude for the justification you have in Christ by faith alone.

REVIEW QUIZ

Use these multiple-choice questions to measure what you learned from this lesson.

1. At the time of Paul's confrontation of Peter, what city was the center of Christianity?
    a. Jerusalem
    b. Rome
    c. Antioch
    d. Galatia

2. What issue was central to Paul's contention with Peter in Antioch?
    a. Circumcision
    b. Feasts
    c. Festivals
    d. Food

3. What title did Paul use when referring to those who pressured Peter to withdraw from gentile believers?
    a. "The circumcision party"
    b. "The Judaizers"
    c. "The Gentiles"
    d. "The Antiochian school"

4. What is the law's pedagogic function?
    a. The law restrains sin.
    b. The law is a guide for sanctification.
    c. The law shows us our sinfulness.
    d. The law set Israel apart as a nation in the Old Testament.

5. What was nailed to the cross?
    a. The person of Christ
    b. Our Adamic identity
    c. Our record of debt
    d. All of the above

6. What is the heart of Paul's theology?
    a. Justification by faith alone
    b. The unity of believers
    c. Union with Christ
    d. The law of God

Answer Key—Paul Opposes Peter

REFLECTION & DISCUSSION QUESTIONS

Before the Video

What Do You Think?

These are personal questions. The answers should be based on your own knowledge and experience.

Scripture Reading

- How do the positive and negative statements in this passage reinforce the doctrine of justification by faith alone in Christ alone?

  Paul leads with the negative assertion that no one is justified by works of the law. He then follows that with the positive statement about a person's being justified by faith in Jesus Christ. Paul reiterates what he has said in positive terms and then closes with two more negative statements about the impossibility of a person's being justified by works of the law. The contrast and reiteration of the negative and positive statements emphasize the doctrine of justification by faith alone in Christ alone.

During the Video

Historical Narrative

- What brought about Peter's change of behavior toward gentile converts in Antioch?

  Peter ate with gentile converts until certain men came to Antioch from Jerusalem. Peter feared these men and withdrew from the gentiles. He succumbed to the pressure of these Jewish visitors. Paul summarized the situation in Galatians 2:12 when he wrote, "Before certain men came from James, he was eating with the Gentiles; but when they came he drew back and separated himself, fearing the circumcision party."

- What were those from Jerusalem implying when they insisted that the gentile converts eat only kosher food?

  By insisting that the gentiles eat only kosher food, the circumcision party was implying that gentiles must become Jews. Peter was essentially cutting the gentile believers off from the family of God by refusing to eat with them. Paul contended that this was equivalent to insisting that faith in Christ is not enough to be saved, and he argued that justification by faith alone was at stake.

Theological Reflection

- What role does obedience to the law play in our justification?

  Our obedience to God's law plays absolutely no part in our justification. Justification is by grace alone through faith alone in Christ alone. However, obedience does play a role in our justification. Jesus had to obey the law of God perfectly for us. While our attempts to obey the law are futile, Jesus' obedience to the law is imputed to us.

- What does Galatians 2:19 teach us about the relationship between our justification and a life of obedience?

  In Galatians 2:19, Paul explained that he died to the law so that he might live to God. We must never reverse the order. We are justified by faith alone in Christ apart from our obedience to the law. However, once we are justified, we seek to live obedient lives before God. Because God has loved us and given His Son for us, He enables us to respond to Him in grateful obedience. If we reverse the order, we destroy the gospel.

After the Video

- What do we learn about the relationship between behavior and belief from Peter's actions?

  By withdrawing from the gentile believers in Antioch, Peter was revealing that he did not truly believe in justification by faith alone. Before the men came from Jerusalem, Peter was eating foods that were unclean according to the Mosaic law. He then stopped eating these foods. However, now that Christ had come and had fulfilled the old covenant ceremonial laws, there was no reason for Peter to observe them. By his actions, Peter was revealing what he really believed about how someone is justified before God.

- Why is it vital for us to understand that union with Christ is the center of Paul's theology?

  In Galatians, Paul explains that union with Christ marks believers' spiritual identity. In Galatians 2:20, he writes, "I have been crucified with Christ." Paul was reflecting on the fact that the old Adamic nature had been crucified in the death of Christ so that the believer is made alive in union with Christ. Paul's primary way of thinking about himself was as a man in union with Christ. He continually uses the phrase "in Christ" in his letters.

- What did Paul mean when he said that "through the law I died to the law"?

  Paul is not saying that there is no more place for the law in the Christian life. He is reflecting on the role of the law in justification. There was a point when Paul was crushed by the law. The demands of the law were too weighty for him. He died to its demands in the death of Jesus, and he died to its threats in union with Christ.

REVIEW QUIZ

Lesson 4

1. **C.**

   At the time of Paul's confrontation of Peter, Antioch was the center of Christianity. The center had formerly been Jerusalem. However, as persecution forced more and more Christians to scatter from Jerusalem, Antioch became a safe haven for many of these Christian refugees. Antioch also became the center of the Apostles' missionary endeavors. The first missionary journey was from Antioch, and every time Paul reported on his journeys, he did so in Antioch.

2. **D.**

   Paul contended with Peter in Antioch over Peter's refusal to eat with gentile converts. For the sake of his outreach to the gentiles, Peter had become accustomed to eating things that were once considered unclean. However, when men came from Jerusalem, Peter withdrew and refused to eat certain foods with the gentiles. This was a functional denial of justification by faith alone.

3. **A.**

   Though the issue in Antioch was over an inappropriate insistence on the observance of Old Testament dietary laws—rather than over circumcision—the same group of people who had contended with Paul over the circumcision of Titus were now pressuring Peter about dietary restrictions. Because of the previous incident, Paul called them "the circumcision party."

4. **C.**

   In its pedagogic function, the law teaches us that we are sinners in need of a Savior. It makes us realize that we have broken all God's commandments and have fallen short of His glory. The Apostle Paul refers to the pedagogic function of the law in Romans 7 when he explains how the law made his sin "sinful beyond measure." Though God requires that we keep the law, the law shows us that we can't keep it, but it helps us realize that we need Jesus to keep it for us.

5. **D.**

   In this lesson, Dr. Thomas explained that Jesus, our old Adamic identity, and our record of debt were all nailed to the cross. In Colossians 2:14, Paul explains that the record of debt that was against us was taken away, having been nailed to the cross. In Galatians 2:20, he says, "I have been crucified with Christ." Paul is referring to his old Adamic nature as crucified in Christ. When Christ died, we died with Him. Our old man was crucified with Christ, and our identity is now entirely based on what has happened to us in the death of Jesus.

6. **C.**

   As central as justification by faith alone is to the gospel, the heart of Paul's theology is union with Christ. The primary way in which Paul speaks about Christians is that they are "in Christ." Paul uses the Greek phrase en Christo *("in Christ") sixty-eight times in his epistles. Paul cannot write Christian theology without mentioning that he used to be in Adam but that now he is in Christ.*

5

The Heart of Galatians

INTRODUCTION

At the heart of the gospel is justification by grace alone through faith alone in Christ alone. In the church in Galatia, the Judaizers sought to lead the members of the church away from the simplicity of this faith in Christ by insisting on law-keeping for their justification. In this lesson, Dr. Thomas walks through the Apostle Paul's great defense of justification by faith alone apart from works of the law.

LEARNING GOALS

When you have finished this lesson, you should be able to:

- Explain the meaning of the phrase "works of the law"
- Understand the contrast between works of the law and faith in Christ
- Identify the central Old Testament example of justification by faith alone
- Summarize Paul's exposition of the demands of the law from Deuteronomy
- Understand how Jesus removes the curse of the law that we are under by nature

KEY IDEAS

- Paul rebukes the members of the church for allowing themselves to be deceived by a false gospel.
- Remembering that we are justified by faith alone is key to our Christian life.
- Justification by faith alone is revealed in the Old Testament Scriptures, specifically through the example of Abraham.
- Christ became a curse for us by suffering in our place on the cross, where He took the guilt of our sin by imputation and fell under the wrath of God.

REFLECTION & DISCUSSION QUESTIONS

Before the Video

What Do You Think?

Take a moment to answer the following questions. They will prepare you for the lecture.

- What is necessary for you to remain faithful as a Christian?

- How have you understood the phrase "works of the law"?

Scripture Reading

O foolish Galatians! Who has bewitched you? It was before your eyes that Jesus Christ was publicly portrayed as crucified. Let me ask you only this: Did you receive the Spirit by works of the law or by hearing with faith? Are you so foolish? Having begun by the Spirit, are you now being perfected by the flesh? Did you suffer so many things in vain—if indeed it was in vain? Does he who supplies the Spirit to you and works miracles among you do so by works of the law, or by hearing with faith—just as Abraham "believed God, and it was counted to him as righteousness"?

—Galatians 3:1–6

- What does this passage reveal about beginning and continuing in the Christian life?

During the Video

Answer the following questions while you watch the video. They will guide you through the lecture.

Means of Justification   *0:00–10:35*

- In this passage, Paul sets out two antithetical ways of being brought into a right relationship with God. What are they?

- Who is the prototype of justification by faith alone?

- How were the Old Testament saints saved?

Depending on Works   *10:35–14:50*

- What does the law require for someone to be justified by it?

- Why does Paul appeal to Habakkuk in Galatians 3:11?

Redemption in Christ   *14:50–23:08*

- What did Jesus have to do to redeem us?

- What concern did Paul address at the beginning of this section regarding the believer's continuing in the Christian life?

After the Video

Answer the following questions after you have finished the lecture. They will help you identify and summarize the major points.

- What does the timing of Abraham's justification in light of his circumcision teach us about the doctrine of justification?

If you are in a group, have the members discuss how we can view religious rituals, such as baptism, improperly in the same way that the Judaizers viewed circumcision.

- What does Westminster Shorter Catechism 84 teach about the relationship between sin and the curse?

If you are in a group, have the members discuss the ways in which we tend to categorize sin. Why do we like to compare ourselves with others? How often do you catch yourself downplaying the severity of your sin while failing to recognize what every sin deserves before God?

- Why can we be certain that God will not pour out His wrath on us if we are in Christ by faith?

If you are in a group, have the members discuss how easily we forget about the satisfaction of God's justice and the propitiation of His wrath in the death of Christ. Consider asking questions such as these: Why is it important for us to remember that there is no more wrath for those who are in Christ Jesus? How does it inform our Christian life and our assurance of salvation?

PRAYER

Commit what you have learned from God's Word in this lesson to prayer.

- Praise God for revealing the one way of salvation in the Old and New Testament.
- Confess the ways that you have downplayed the severity of what you consider to be small sins.
- Thank God that Jesus Christ was born under the law and suffered its curse to deliver you from His wrath.
- Ask God to help you see your need to continue living the Christian life by faith in Jesus Christ and His finished work.

REVIEW QUIZ

Use these multiple-choice questions to measure what you learned from this lesson.

1. According to Dr. Thomas, how were the Judaizers viewing the "works of the law"?
   a. As means by which one could merit a right standing before God
   b. As markers by which gentiles were included in the covenant community
   c. As a method to dietary health
   d. As a mode of civil righteousness

2. The story of the gospel begins in the New Testament with Jesus.
   a. True
   b. False

3. What does the term *counted* mean in Greek?
   a. "Infused"
   b. "Imputed"
   c. "Imparted"
   d. "Included"

4. What does the phrase *simul justus et peccator* mean?
   a. "Like an unjust sinner"
   b. "Justified and no longer sinful"
   c. "At the same time justified and a sinner"
   d. "Instantaneously just on account of faith"

5. How much of the law would a person have to obey in order to be justified by the works of the law?
   a. None of it
   b. 100 percent
   c. 51 percent or more
   d. As much as one can possibly obey

6. What was the gospel of the Judaizers?
   a. A gospel of grace
   b. A gospel of inclusion
   c. A gospel of circumcision
   d. A gospel of "try harder"

Answer Key—The Heart of Galatians

REFLECTION & DISCUSSION QUESTIONS

Before the Video

What Do You Think?

> *These are personal questions. The answers should be based on your own knowledge and experience.*

Scripture Reading

- What does this passage reveal about beginning and continuing in the Christian life?

  Paul opens this passage with a strong rebuke of the believers in Galatia because he saw that they were falling into the trap of believing that the Christian life begins by faith but continues by works. They had wrongly adopted a "get in by grace; stay in by works" mentality.

During the Video

Means of Justification

- In this passage, Paul sets out two antithetical ways of being brought into a right relationship with God. What are they?

  The two antithetical ways of being accepted by God, as described in this passage, are "works of the law" and "hearing by faith." Of course, Paul is setting these two ways of justification in contrast because it is impossible for someone to be justified by works of the law. The gospel teaches that justification is by faith alone in Christ alone.

- Who is the prototype of justification by faith alone?

  Abraham, the central father figure for the Jewish people, is the prototype of justification by faith alone. Genesis 15:6 teaches us that Abraham was justified by faith alone. Moses writes, "He believed the LORD, and he counted it to him as righteousness." Abraham believed the promise of God that he would have a son in whom the nations would be blessed, and he received the righteousness of God by faith alone.

- How were the Old Testament saints saved?

  The Old Testament saints were saved in exactly the same way that new covenant believers are saved: by faith alone. In Romans 4, the Apostle Paul appeals to the example of Abraham and David. In Genesis 15:6, Abraham is said to have believed the promise of the gospel and was counted righteous by God. There is no difference in the way that God worked to redeem His people in the Old and New Testaments.

Depending on Works

- What does the law require for someone to be justified by it?

  If the law is to be kept, it requires perfect obedience. In Galatians 3:10, Paul cites Deuteronomy 27:26 and writes, "Cursed be everyone who does not abide by all things written in the Book of the Law, and do them." If someone could be justified by the law, he would have to keep the law in all its fullness.

- Why does Paul appeal to Habakkuk in Galatians 3:11?

  Citing Habakkuk 2:4, Paul explains, "Now it is evident that no one is justified before God by the law, for 'The righteous shall live by faith.'" He cites it is to prove that the whole of the Christian life is lived by faith. We are counted righteous at the beginning of our Christian life by faith alone, and we will continue to be counted righteous by faith alone when we die.

Redemption in Christ

- What did Jesus have to do to redeem us?

  According to Galatians 3:13, Jesus had to become a curse for us in order to redeem us. Since we were by nature under the curse of the law of God because of our disobedience, Christ was born under the law to do what we could not do for ourselves. Jesus perfectly obeyed God's law for us. He never sinned. Jesus then took the wrath of God that we deserve because of our failure to keep God's law perfectly. Our sins were imputed to Christ, and God cursed Him on the cross. He was forsaken so that we, through faith, might be counted righteous in Him.

- What concern did Paul address at the beginning of this section regarding the believer's continuing in the Christian life?

  The Apostle was concerned that the members of the church had allowed themselves to be deceived by the Judaizers to believe that the beginning of the Christian life is by faith and the rest of the Christian life is by obedience. Rather than holding fast to the idea that we are motivated to obedience by our justification, the Judaizers taught that we could complete in the flesh what was begun by the Spirit. This was a denial of the doctrine of justification by faith alone.

After the Video

- What does the timing of Abraham's justification in light of his circumcision teach us about the doctrine of justification?

  It is extremely important for us to see that the Scripture teaches that Abraham was justified by faith alone in Genesis 15:6 before being circumcised in Genesis 17. If our justification before God were dependent on our observation of the ceremonial laws—circumcision being the first of these laws—then Abraham would have been justified after he was circumcised. The Apostle Paul makes this point in Romans 4:10.

- What does Westminster Shorter Catechism 84 teach about the relationship between sin and the curse?

  Westminster Shorter Catechism 84 teaches us that "every sin deserves God's wrath and curse." Though some sins are more heinous than others, there is no sin that does not deserve the righteous judgment of God. This is Paul's point in appealing to Leviticus and Deuteronomy in Galatians 3:10: "For all who rely on works of the law are under a curse; for it is written, 'Cursed be everyone who does not abide by all things written in the Book of the Law, and do them.'"

- Why can we be certain that God will not pour out His wrath on us if we are in Christ by faith?

  Since Jesus was forsaken by God and made a curse in our place, we can rest assured that God will not change and decide to pour out His wrath on us. God is not like the gods of the Romans or the Greeks. He is not duplicitous. He is just and righteous. Because Jesus died under the wrath of God for us, God's wrath has been propitiated and His justice satisfied.

REVIEW QUIZ

Lesson 5

1. **A.**

   The Judaizers viewed the ceremonial laws as a boundary markers by which a person could claim merit in the sight of God. The "works of the law" were, accordingly, means by which a person could perform before God in such a way as to enable him to merit a right standing with God.

2. **B.**

   Though many mistakenly believe that the gospel begins with the incarnation of Jesus, Dr. Thomas made the important point that the story of the gospel began in the Old Testament. The narrative of the gospel goes back to the beginning, and God also gave Abraham the gospel promise. In Galatians 3:8, we read, "And the Scripture, foreseeing that God would justify the Gentiles by faith, preached the gospel beforehand to Abraham."

3. **B.**

   The word translated "counted" in many English translations of the Bible comes from the Greek word that means "imputed." This word may also rightly be translated "credited." It is an accounting term. It carries the idea of a plus column. Jesus' righteousness is counted, imputed, or credited to the believer in the same way that it was credited to Abraham. Believers are legally and federally righteous before God by the imputed righteousness of Christ.

4. **C.**

   Martin Luther often used the phrase simul justus et peccator *to explain the dual reality for believers in this life. The Christian is simultaneously justified and a sinner. Justification does not morally transform a person. It puts him in a right standing before God. It makes a person legally righteous in the law court of God. At the same time, the Christian is still a wretched sinner in this life.*

5. **B.**

   If a person could be saved by law-keeping, the law would have to be kept perfectly: "Cursed be everyone who does not abide by all things written in the Book of the Law, and do them" (Gal. 3:10). As Dr. Thomas explained, "It is all or nothing. You have to obey all of the law. You have to obey all the law in terms of its breadth, and you have to obey the law in terms of its extent and depth."

6. **D.**

   The gospel of the Judaizers was a gospel of "try harder." They were calling to members of the church in Galatia to do more in order to gain a right standing with God. By so doing, they were not teaching a gospel at all. The false gospel of "try harder" always leads to despair. It tells people to seek for their assurance and peace by pulling themselves up by their bootstraps.

6

Law & Promise

INTRODUCTION

The Judaizers were propagating a false gospel among the members of the church in Galatia by insisting that gentile converts needed to keep the Jewish ceremonial law for their justification before God. In response, the Apostle Paul explained that Abraham, the father of the faith, was justified by faith alone. In this lesson, Dr. Thomas expounds on the Apostle Paul's teaching about the relationship between the promise God gave to Abraham and the law He gave to Israel.

LEARNING GOALS

When you have finished this lesson, you should be able to:

- Explain the relationship between the promise of God and the law of God
- Recognize the importance of the chronology associated with the giving of the promise and the giving of the law
- Understand the three uses of the law

KEY IDEAS

- No one will be justified before God by law-keeping, since justification is by faith alone in the promised Messiah.
- The law, which God gave to Moses given 430 years after He gave the promise to Abraham, cannot annul or add to the promise.
- In the context of how a person is justified before God, the law is useful only in showing us our sinfulness and our need for a Savior, in restraining sin, and in guiding Christians on how to live godly lives.

REFLECTION & DISCUSSION QUESTIONS

Before the Video

What Do You Think?

Take a moment to answer the following questions. They will prepare you for the lecture.

- Why would someone have trouble understanding that God's promise to Abraham is for all believers and not simply for Israel?

- If no one can be justified by the law, why did God give the law to His people?

Scripture Reading

The promises were made to Abraham and to his offspring. It does not say, "And to off-springs," referring to many, but referring to one, "And to your offspring," who is Christ.

—Galatians 3:16

- What does this passage reveal about the divinely intended recipients of the promise of God?

During the Video

Answer the following questions while you watch the video. They will guide you through the lecture.

The Law and Justification   *0:00–13:40*

- How can Abraham be the father of the faith for gentiles?

- How does the story of the Old Testament apply to gentile believers?

- Why does Paul point out the chronology of the giving of the promise and the giving of the law? How does he defend the idea that Abraham was justified by faith and not by law-keeping?

The Purpose of the Law   *13:40–22:47*

- What are the three uses of the law of God?

- How does Galatians 3:22 promote a pedagogic use of the law?

After the Video

Answer the following questions after you have finished the lecture. They will help you identify and summarize the major points.

- Martin Luther once made a statement that many people have considered "the most perfect expression of the relationship between law and gospel." What was it?

  If you are in a group, have the members discuss the importance of keeping these two things together in the Christian life. What are some ways that we fail to keep them in sequence?

- What illustration did Dr. Thomas give to explain the binding nature of the promissory aspect of a covenant?

  If you are in a group, have the members discuss how we ought to find comfort and assurance in the fact that God's promise is binding. What difference should this truth make to our lives?

- What are some of the ways that we wrongly seek to make our justification more certain?

  If you are in a group, have the members discuss their own experience in this regard. Ask them to elaborate on the other ways that they may seek more assurance of their justification before God by the things they do.

PRAYER

Commit what you have learned from God's Word in this lesson to prayer.

- Praise God for the binding nature of His covenant promise.
- Confess times when you have tried to secure justification in your experience by things you do.
- Thank God for the assurance we have of the certainty of the promise based on the finished work of Christ.
- Ask God to give you a greater understanding of your ongoing need for the gospel.

REVIEW QUIZ

Use these multiple-choice questions to measure what you learned from this lesson.

1. What promise that God made with Abraham does Paul appeal to in Galatians 3:16?
    a. That Abraham would have a son
    b. That Abraham would have many sons
    c. That Abraham would be the father of a nation
    d. All of the above

2. Why is Paul's emphasis on Abraham in Galatians 3 important for gentiles?
    a. It teaches them to accept a Jewish identity.
    b. It situates them in the new covenant promises.
    c. It commends to them the practice of circumcision.
    d. It shows them how they are a part of the story of the Old Testament.

3. How many years passed between the giving of the promise and the giving of the law?
    a. 400
    b. 430
    c. 480
    d. 500

4. What most closely describes the three uses of the law?
    a. As a moral law, civil law, and ceremonial law
    b. As civil restraint, pedagogic law, and ceremonial law
    c. As moral restraint, ceremonial law, and pedagogic law
    d. As civil restraint, pedagogic law, and guide for obedience

5. How did Jesus respond to the rich young ruler's question, "What good deed must I do to have eternal life?"
    a. He told him to believe.
    b. He drove him to the law.
    c. He didn't answer him.
    d. He explained the gospel to him.

6. In Romans 7, the Apostle explains that one of the Ten Commandments helped him see his sinfulness. What commandment was it?
    a. "You shall not covet."
    b. "You shall have no other gods before me."
    c. "You shall not commit adultery."
    d. "You shall not murder."

Answer Key—Law & Promise

REFLECTION & DISCUSSION QUESTIONS

Before the Video

What Do You Think?

These are personal questions. The answers should be based on your own knowledge and experience.

Scripture Reading

- What does this passage reveal about the divinely intended recipients of the promise of God?

   The Lord gave the promise of the everlasting inheritance to Abraham and his offspring. Though an initial reading of this verse seems to suggest that the promise was also given to Abraham and his physical descendants, the Apostle Paul explains that God gave it to Abraham and to his singular offspring, who is Christ. In Christ, all believers receive the promise of the everlasting inheritance because that promise is fulfilled in Jesus Christ.

During the Video

The Law and Justification

- How can Abraham be the father of the faith for gentiles?

   The promise that God gave Abraham was dependent on his having a son. This promised son was ultimately Jesus Christ. In Galatians 3:16, Paul explains that God gave the promise of the inheritance to Abraham and to his offspring, who is Christ. Jesus fulfills the promise given to Abraham so that Abraham is now the spiritual father of all who have the faith of Abraham, whether Jew or gentile.

- How does the story of the Old Testament apply to gentile believers?

   In the lesson, Dr. Thomas explained that the narrative of the gospel runs through the Old Testament, going all the way back to Abraham. Since Abraham believed the same gospel that the gentiles had come to believe, this makes the story of the Old Testament as much a part of the believing gentiles' history as it is for the physical descendants of Abraham.

- Why does Paul point out the chronology of the giving of the promise and the giving of the law? How does he defend the idea that Abraham was justified by faith and not by law-keeping?

   In Galatians 3:17, Paul explains that Abraham received the promises of God by faith in the promised Messiah and that he was therefore justified by faith alone

430 years before the giving of the law at Sinai. Paul is contrasting two covenantal dealings of God—the first a covenant of promise and the second the giving of the law. The law cannot change the promise. It cannot set the promise aside. The promise remains free from any insistence that one keep the law to gain the promise. Because the promise was given to Abraham 430 years before the giving of the law, justification was always by faith alone.

The Purpose of the Law

- What are the three uses of the law of God?

  The first of the three uses of the law is a civil use: the law restrains evil, and it has purpose in society. It brings stability to society by maintaining order. Second, the law has a pedagogic use: the law was given by God to point out the contours of sin and was given 430 years after the promise "because of transgressions" (Gal. 3:19), so it helps us see our sinfulness and our need of the Savior. In regard to justification, this makes it useful in driving men to Christ for redemption and forgiveness. Third, the law has a use in the process of our sanctification: the law provides the pattern of obedience for those who have been justified. Since believers have been crucified with Christ and have been raised to newness of life, the law guides them in how they are to live for God.

- How does Galatians 3:22 promote a pedagogic use of the law?

  In verse 22, Paul says that "the Scripture imprisoned everything under sin, so that the promise by faith in Jesus Christ might be given to those who believe." The law imprisons the unregenerate. Paul may be speaking from his own experience before his conversion, or he may be speaking about the redemptive-historical difference between the Old and New Testaments. It is likely that he has the latter in view. Regardless, the law here serves the purpose of imprisoning sinners so that they will see their need for the promised Redeemer.

After the Video

- Martin Luther once made a statement that many people have considered "the most perfect expression of the relationship between law and gospel." What was it?

  In On the Babylonian Captivity of the Church, *Luther wrote, "A Christian is an utterly free man, lord of all and subject to none; a Christian is an utterly dutiful man, servant of all and subject to all." The point is that believers have been set free from the demands and threats of the law by the gospel. We are not justified by the law. We have been set free from the demands of the law for our justification. We have also been set free from the threats of the law. However, we are not free from the obligations to obey God's commandments out of gratitude. We desire to obey God by the aid of the Holy Spirit because we have become the recipients of His grace.*

- What illustration did Dr. Thomas give to explain the binding nature of the promissory aspect of a covenant?

  Dr. Thomas told the story of a woman who had died and left half her inheritance to the church and half to a distant relative. This relative wanted more than the half of what she had been promised in the will. This distant relative went to a lawyer to see whether she could profit more than what she had been contractually promised. The lawyer charged her one thousand dollars for his labors and gave her the rest of the half of the promised inheritance. This illustrates the binding nature of the covenant promise. The Apostle Paul explains in Galatians 3:15 that even human covenants have a binding element to their promises. No one can take away from them and no one can add to them. God's promise to Abraham is firm and immovable.

- What are some of the ways that we wrongly seek to make our justification more certain?

  In the lesson, Dr. Thomas explained that we default to seeking assurance of justification by things that we do. When we are not doing well spiritually, we may try to convince ourselves that we will be justified before God by praying more or by being kinder to others. There is, in all of us, a tendency to think that we start the Christian life by the gospel but that we continue in the flesh. The Apostle Paul teaches that this is contrary to the gospel.

REVIEW QUIZ

Lesson 6

1. **D.**

   In Galatians 3:16, the Apostle Paul explained that the promise made to Abraham was to him and to his offspring, who is Christ. The promise relates to the son God promised Abraham, but it also relates to the fact that God promised to make Abraham a great nation and that he would have many sons, even among the gentiles. The whole promise to Abraham is dependent on its fulfillment in the Son, Jesus Christ.

2. **D.**

   The promise that God gave to Abraham was the promise of the gospel that extended to all the nations. Because of the promise given to Abraham, gentile believers can understand themselves as the spiritual sons of Abraham in Christ and have every right to see themselves as part of the story of the Old Testament.

3. **B.**

   A period of 430 years passed between the covenant God made with Abraham and the giving of the law at Sinai. This is important because the law cannot set aside or add to the promise. The promise stands because it was given first. The law cannot change the promise in any way whatsoever.

4. **D.**

The law is used as a civil restraint of sin, as a pedagogical mirror to expose sin and lead one to Christ, and as a guide for obedience in the Christian life. Though Paul has the pedagogic use of the law in view in this section of Galatians—because he is dealing with the subject of justification—the other uses of the law are supported by Scripture, and Paul will touch on the law's use in the Christian life later in this letter.

5. **B.**

When the rich young ruler came to Jesus asking, "What good deed must I do to have eternal life?" Jesus didn't tell him to believe. Though one is not saved by the law, Jesus pointed this man to the law so that he might be able to see his sinfulness and need for the Savior. This man had no sense of his need for Christ. He thought he was alive, but he was spiritually dead.

6. **A.**

In Romans 7:7, Paul writes, "I would not have known what it is to covet if the law had not said, 'You shall not covet.'" Paul explains that the tenth commandment exposed his covetous heart. The pedagogical purpose of the law is to expose our sinfulness so that we will be crushed under it and that we will, in turn, see our need for the Savior. The law brings our sinfulness into focus.

7

Sons & Heirs

INTRODUCTION

Throughout the letter to the Galatians, the Apostle Paul has been defending the gospel and the doctrine of justification by faith alone. Having defended justification by faith alone from the example of Abraham, Paul now turns his attention to the blessing of adoption. In this lecture, Dr. Thomas focuses on the teaching of Galatians 3:23–4:7 and on the difference between the experience of the people of God in the old and new covenants.

LEARNING GOALS

When you have finished this lesson, you should be able to:

- Explain the two administrations of the gospel
- Understand the way in which the law functioned as a tutor in the old covenant
- Recognize why adoption is the chief blessing of the gospel
- Identify the promised inheritance

KEY IDEAS

- God kept His people under the old covenant law as a guardian until Christ came.
- Christ came into the world to fulfill the promises made to Abraham.
- The greatest blessing of the gospel is adoption as sons into the family of God.
- All those who have faith in Christ are sons of Abraham and heirs of the promise.
- God has promised that all His children will inherit the new heavens and the new earth.

REFLECTION & DISCUSSION QUESTIONS

Before the Video

What Do You Think?

Take a moment to answer the following questions. They will prepare you for the lecture.

- What is your understanding of the difference between the old covenant and the new covenant? How are they similar? How do they differ?

- Who is the offspring of Abraham?

Scripture Reading

When the fullness of time had come, God sent forth his Son, born of woman, born under the law, to redeem those who were under the law, so that we might receive adoption as sons.

—Galatians 4:4–5

- Why did Jesus have to be born under the law to redeem those who were under the law?

During the Video

Answer the following questions while you watch the video. They will guide you through the lecture.

Coming of Age   *0:00–7:51*

- Why does Paul liken the old covenant law to a tutor?

- What does Paul mean when he says, "The heir, as long as he is a child, is no different from a slave" (Gal. 4:1)?

Age of the Spirit   *7:51–25:53*

- Why does Paul stress that Christ was born of a woman?

- What is the chief blessing of the gospel?

After the Video

Answer the following questions after you have finished the lecture. They will help you identify and summarize the major points.

- What does Paul mean when he writes, "There is no male and female, for you are all one in Christ Jesus" (Gal. 3:28)?

    If you are in a group, have the members discuss the way that the gospel brings equal blessings to all believers irrespective of gender, ethnicity, or nationality.

- What is the trajectory of salvation history?

    If you are in a group, have the members discuss what effect this truth ought to have on our Christian lives. What is the result of failing to realize this reality?

- How does God assure us of our sonship?

    If you are in a group, have the members read Romans 8:16–17. Ask them questions such as these: How does the Spirit assure us of our adoption as sons of God? How often do you pray for the assurance of sonship?

PRAYER

Commit what you have learned from God's Word in this lesson to prayer.

- Praise God for the blessing of adoption.
- Confess the ways that you have acted more like a slave than a son.
- Thank God for securing an everlasting inheritance for you by grace.
- Ask God to give you a greater measure of assurance of your adoption.

REVIEW QUIZ

Use these multiple-choice questions to measure what you learned from this lesson.

1. In Galatians, who does Paul argue are the children of Abraham in the new covenant?
    a. All mankind
    b. The gentiles who convert to Judaism
    c. Jews and gentiles who believe in Jesus
    d. The physical descendants of Abraham

2. In Galatians 3:16, who is the "offspring" of Abraham?
   a. Isaac
   b. The Israelites
   c. New covenant believers
   d. Christ

3. What does the phrase "the elementary principles of the world" likely mean in Galatians 4:3 and 4:9?
   a. Pagan practices
   b. Natural law
   c. The fundamentals of Christianity
   d. The minutiae of the law

4. To what does Paul refer when he speaks of "the fullness of time" in Galatians 4:4?
   a. The fulfillment of the Abrahamic promise
   b. The building of Romans roads throughout the world
   c. The period of the spread of the Greek language
   d. All of the above

5. Why does Paul stress that Christ was "born of woman"?
   a. To emphasize Jesus' sinless nature
   b. To emphasize Jesus' humanity
   c. To emphasize the fulfillment of Genesis 3:15
   d. All of the above

6. What will believers ultimately inherit because they have received adoption into the family of God by faith in Christ?
   a. The land of Israel
   b. This present world
   c. The new heavens and new earth
   d. The promised Holy Spirit

Answer Key—Sons & Heirs

Before the Video

What Do You Think?

> *These are personal questions. The answers should be based on your own knowledge and experience.*

Scripture Reading

- Why did Jesus have to be born under the law to redeem those who were under the law?

> *Jesus had to be born under the law to fulfill the demands of the law for those who would believe in Him. He had to come under the curse of the law. Jesus was born under the law to deliver all of us who are by nature under the curse of the law in Adam.*

During the Video

Coming of Age

- Why does Paul liken the old covenant law to a tutor?

> *The old covenant law was like a guardian or tutor until Christ came. It served a purpose in salvation history. Going back to the old covenant era would be like going backward in maturation. The Judaizers were trying to put Christians under the bondage and imprisonment of the old covenant. Paul wanted believers to know that this is not the trajectory of salvation history. Rather, salvation history moves from adolescence to adulthood.*

- What does Paul mean when he says, "The heir, as long as he is a child, is no different from a slave" (Gal. 4:1)?

> *To teach the need for Christ and the gospel, the old covenant, in comparison with the new covenant, functioned as a period of bondage and death. The law kept God's people in check to show them how sinful they were and how much they needed the promised Savior. In this sense, one could not tell the difference between a child and a slave in the experience of the old covenant.*

Age of the Spirit

- Why does Paul stress that Christ was born of a woman?

> *Jesus had to be born of a woman to fulfill the promise of Genesis 3:15. He is the long-awaited offspring of the woman. He is also the long-awaited offspring of*

*Abraham. The offspring promised to Adam and Eve is the same offspring prom-
ised to Abraham. Additionally, Jesus had to be born of a woman and born under
the law to fulfill its demands and take its curse on our behalf.*

- What is the chief blessing of the gospel?

  *The chief blessing of the gospel is not justification. The chief blessing of the gospel is
  our adoption as sons of God. When we receive adoption, we are brought into the family of God, and Jesus becomes our elder brother. We also become brothers and sisters
  of one another in Christ, and we become heirs of all that belongs to our Father.*

After the Video

- What does Paul mean when he writes, "There is no male and female, for you are
  all one in Christ Jesus" (Gal. 3:28)?

  *When Paul says that there is no male or female in Christ, he is not suggesting that
  there are no more gender distinctions. Rather, he is teaching that both male and
  female share the same privileges in the gospel. Dr. Thomas explained, "There is
  absolute and total equality as far as the gospel is concerned." No other world reli-
  gions teach what the New Testament does in this regard.*

- What is the trajectory of salvation history?

  *The trajectory of salvation history is from adolescence to maturity. This trajec-
  tory can be seen in Paul's analogy: just as children learn in schools under a tutor,
  so God put His people under the law in order to teach them their need for Christ.
  Once Christ came, there was no need for the tutor, for those who have faith in Him
  have reached maturity, and having received Him, they are heirs by God's grace
  through faith alone.*

- How does God assure us of our sonship?

  *Just as the Spirit of God upheld Jesus and assured Him of His Sonship, so He
  indwells believers and assures us of our adoption into God's family. In Galatians
  4:6, Paul writes, "Because you are sons, God has sent the Spirit of his Son into our
  hearts, crying, 'Abba! Father!'" The Holy Spirit bears witness with our spirit and
  assures us of our position as sons to assure us that we have a right to the everlasting inheritance. Paul uses the word "son" to intimate that we are heirs of the
  inheritance in Christ.*

REVIEW QUIZ

Lesson 7

1. **C.**

   *The children of Abraham in the new covenant are all those who believe in Christ—
   whether Jew or gentile. Paul says, "And if you are Christ's, then you are Abraham's
   offspring, heirs according to promise" (Gal. 3:29). In saying this, Paul is especially*

interested in assuring gentile believers that the old covenant heritage is their own heritage through faith in Christ. They are no less the children of Abraham than believing Jews.

2. **D.**

   In salvation history, the offspring of Abraham is Christ. In Galatians 3:16, Paul wrote, "The promises were made to Abraham and to his offspring. It does not say, 'And to offsprings,' referring to many, but referring to one, 'And to your offspring,' who is Christ." God made promises to Abraham that were passed down to Christ to fulfill. In this sense, it is not Isaac or Israel who is the offspring of Abraham, but the Redeemer.

3. **D.**

   In Galatians 4:3 and 4:9, Paul refers to "the elementary principles of the world." He speaks of them as enslaving principles from which Christ came and died to set believers free. In this context, Paul seems to be talking about the minutiae of the law that God gave the old covenant community in order to help them understand the basics of religion and to drive them to Christ for redemption.

4. **A.**

   Though the worldwide implementation of Roman roads and the spread of the Greek language were enormous blessings for the spread of the gospel across Europe, Paul speaks of "the fullness of time" as the time of the fulfillment of the old covenant promises in the coming of Christ. All of God's purposes in salvation history were fulfilled in Christ. This is especially true in this context of the promises made to Abraham.

5. **C.**

   That Jesus was "born of woman" highlights both His sinless nature and His true humanity; however, in the context of Galatians 4, the reference to His being born of a woman is a redemptive-historical reflection on the fact that He had come into the world as the Redeemer who was promised in Genesis 3:15. The offspring that God had promised to Abraham was the same offspring of promise.

6. **C.**

   All those who have received adoption as sons of God will one day inherit the new heavens and the new earth. We will be coheirs of all things with Christ. God has already given that inheritance to us by His promise, which is confirmed to us by the Holy Spirit (Eph. 1:13–14). Having the Holy Spirit already, we will one day receive the inheritance in all its fullness in glory.

8

The Cost of Legalism

INTRODUCTION

The gospel brings believers into a state of blessedness and produces joy in their lives. When joy is lacking in our lives, it is an indication that we have embraced a legalistic view of the Christian life. In this lesson, Dr. Thomas considers the Apostle Paul's analysis of the symptoms, diagnosis, and treatment of the legalism into which the members of the churches in Galatia had fallen.

LEARNING GOALS

When you have finished this lesson, you should be able to:

- Recognize the marks of legalism
- Know how to properly define *legalism*
- Identify the particular form of legalism that infected the churches in Galatia
- Understand the biblical cure to legalism

KEY IDEAS

- Joylessness is one of the chief evidences of the belief that Christianity mainly consists of duties and rules.
- Legalism seeks to secure our justification before God on the basis of our obedience to His moral law, man-made rules, or any other code of conduct.
- The cure to legalism is to remember what Jesus has done for us and who we are in Him.

REFLECTION & DISCUSSION QUESTIONS

Before the Video

What Do You Think?

> Take a moment to answer the following questions. They will prepare you for the lecture.

- What characteristics mark the lives of those who have become the recipients of God's grace in Christ?

- What is the result when you seek to live the Christian life mainly out of a sense of duty?

Scripture Reading

> *Now that you have come to know God, or rather to be known by God, how can you turn back again to the weak and worthless elementary principles of the world, whose slaves you want to be once more? You observe days and months and seasons and years! I am afraid I may have labored over you in vain.*
>
> —Galatians 4:9–11

- What contrast did Paul make between true Christianity and the legalism into which the Galatians had fallen?

During the Video

> Answer the following questions while you watch the video. They will guide you through the lecture.

Symptoms   *0:00–13:22*

- According to Galatians 4:15, what is the main symptom of legalism?

- We can fall into legalism in a number of subtle ways. What are they?

Diagnosis   *13:22–17:00*

- What is legalism?

• In what way is legalism instinctive within us?

Cure *17:00–22:45*

• What is the counterfeit cure for legalism?

• What is the biblical cure for legalism?

After the Video

Answer the following questions after you have finished the lecture. They will help you identify and summarize the major points.

• How is adherence to the ceremonial law for justification equivalent to idolatry?

If you are in a group, have the members discuss various enslaving forms of idolatry. Encourage them to talk about how to identify these forms of idolatry in their lives.

• In what ways can we erroneously seek to secure our justification by our repentance?

If you are in a group, have the members talk about our inclination to make the quality of our repentance the basis of our justification or the basis of our continuing in a state of justification. Consider asking questions such as this: What effect does this have on your assurance of salvation?

• What is the difference between Paul's saying, "Become as I am," and the Judaizers' trying to get the gentile converts to become like them?

If you are in a group, have the members discuss how easily those in positions of spiritual leadership can abuse their authority by binding the consciences of believers who sincerely want to please the Lord. Consider asking questions such as these: Have you experienced the unbiblical binding of your conscience by a spiritual leader? How do you recognize when this is happening?

PRAYER

Commit what you have learned from God's Word in this lesson to prayer.

• Praise God for the joy He has given us in Christ.

- Confess the ways in which you have allowed yourself to be enslaved to legalistic counterfeit gospels.
- Thank God for opening your eyes to the understanding that your justification is not based on anything you do.
- Ask God for a deeper understanding of what Christ has done for you and to make you know who you are in Christ.

REVIEW QUIZ

Use these multiple-choice questions to measure what you learned from this lesson.

1. What were the Judaizers saying that gentile converts had to observe?
   a. The moral law of God
   b. The civil law of God
   c. The ceremonial law of God
   d. Man-made rules and regulations

2. What was the purpose of the old covenant ceremonial laws?
   a. To encourage spiritual discipline
   b. To foster national zeal in Israel
   c. To encourage dietary health
   d. To show God's people their need for Christ

3. The Apostle Paul opposed the idea that we need to obey the Ten Commandments.
   a. True
   b. False

4. According to Dr. Thomas, what is *not* included in a definition of *legalism*?
   a. Any sense of obligation to obey God's law in order to be justified
   b. Any sense of obligation to obey man-made rules and regulations
   c. Any sense of obligation to obey God's law for sanctification
   d. Any sense of obligation to obey the ceremonial law of God

5. What is preparationism?
   a. The idea that we need to prepare ourselves for suffering
   b. The idea that we need to prepare ourselves for sanctification
   c. The idea that we need to prepare ourselves for sickness
   d. The idea that we need to prepare ourselves for salvation

6. What was Paul referring to when he told the Galatians, "Become as I am"?
   a. His being an Apostle
   b. His being crucified with Christ
   c. His being a man of strength
   d. His being a Jewish convert

Answer Key—The Cost of Legalism

Before the Video

What Do You Think?

These are personal questions. The answers should be based on your own knowledge and experience.

Scripture Reading

- What contrast did Paul make between true Christianity and the legalism into which the Galatians had fallen?

  According to Paul, Christianity isn't based on following a set of rules and regulations. We do not become Christians because of what we do. Rather, we are Christians because of what God has done for us and in us through Christ. Christ sets His people free from the bondage of sin and the law. Legalism brings people back into the bondage of never-ending performance.

During the Video

Symptoms

- According to Galatians 4:15, what is the main symptom of legalism?

  The main symptom of legalism is seen in Paul's question to the Galatians about their loss of joy and blessedness. They lost their joy because they had begun to think of the Christian life merely in terms of duty. They began to view the Christian faith in terms of a burdensome set of rules to be kept. Though keeping God's commandments is a mark of sincere saving faith, the belief that our law-keeping makes us Christians leads to a burdensome slavery of legalism.

- We can fall into legalism in a number of subtle ways. What are they?

  A major way that legalism creeps into our lives, according to Dr. Thomas, is our putting measurements on how much joy, repentance, and obedience we are experiencing. If we start to ask whether we are experiencing enough joy or repentance, then Christianity becomes a burdensome treadmill. When we start to think that Christianity is primarily about our ability and our continuing to keep God's law, we have fallen into the snare of legalism.

Diagnosis

- What is legalism?

    Legalism is seeking to obey the moral law of God for our justification. It is also any assertion that we must obey man-made laws and rules in order to be justified before God. The particular form of legalism in Galatia, against which Paul wrote, was the Judaizers' insistence that Christian converts must obey old covenant ceremonial laws.

- In what way is legalism instinctive within us?

    We all have difficulty resting in the fact that everything we have spiritually is a free gift of God. We struggle to grasp the freeness of the grace of God in the gospel and seem to be innately tempted toward legalistic approaches to Christianity. We like to convince ourselves that we have to do something to earn or secure the privilege of being set free by Christ and made a child of God.

Cure

- What is the counterfeit cure for legalism?

    Many believe that legalism can be corrected by antinomianism. However, adopting a "take it easy" attitude is not the cure for legalism. In a similar way, those who believe in the continuing validity of the moral law—and in the necessity of sanctification in the believer's life—can fall into the opposite trap of thinking that legalism is the cure to antinomianism. Legalism is not cured by lawlessness, and lawlessness is not cured by legalism. The gospel is the cure for both.

- What is the biblical cure for legalism?

    The cure for legalism is Jesus Christ. We need to remember who Jesus is; what He has done for us in His life, death, and resurrection; and who we are in Christ. The Apostle Paul gives this as the cure to the members of the churches in Galatia when he writes, "Brothers, I entreat you, become as I am, for I also have become as you are" (Gal. 4:12). Paul was not seeking to be justified by observing the Jewish ceremonial law. Rather, he says in Galatians 2:19–20: "Through the law I died to the law, so that I might live to God. I have been crucified with Christ. It is no longer I who live, but Christ who lives in me."

After the Video

- How is adherence to the ceremonial law for justification equivalent to idolatry?

    The heart of sin is idolatry. Whenever we sin, we are worshiping something other than God. The members of the churches in Galatia had fallen into a form of idolatry that centered on making old covenant ceremonial laws the basis of their Christianity. Paul summed up the slavery of this form of idolatry when he wrote, "You observe days and months and seasons and years" (Gal. 4:10).

- In what ways can we erroneously seek to secure our justification by our repentance?

  Although we must repent of our sins before God, our repentance is not what makes us a Christian. Repentance is not the basis of our acceptance by God. When we focus our attention on the quality of our repentance—asking whether we have adequately forsaken sin—we run the risk of believing that our repentance justifies us.

- What is the difference between Paul's saying, "Become as I am," and the Judaizers' trying to get the gentile converts to become like them?

  Paul explained that the Judaizers wanted to shut out the gentile converts out of a desire to make much of themselves. The Judaizers were driven by a zeal for recognition and power. They wanted to lord their requirements over the people. The same can be true in our day. Many in ministry lord over the people their rules and regulations out of a desire to be praised and recognized for their spiritual authority.

REVIEW QUIZ

Lesson 8

1. **C.**

   The Judaizers were calling the gentile converts in the churches in Galatia to specifically observe the old covenant ceremonial laws that God gave to Israel. They were pressing a need for new covenant converts to commit themselves to a life of adherence to the dietary laws, feasts and festivals, and circumcision. In doing so, they were implying that these laws were necessary to the believer's acceptance by God.

2. **D.**

   God gave the people of Israel the old covenant ceremonial laws to show them their sinfulness, to reveal to them their need for salvation, and to point them to the coming Redeemer. Christ fulfilled the ceremonial law as part of His saving work of delivering His people from their bondage. For the Judaizers to insist that new covenant believers need to keep the ceremonial law is to bring them into spiritual bondage, from which Christ has set them free.

3. **B.**

   While Paul stood against maintaining aspects of the ceremonial law for the sake of justification, he was not opposed to obedience to the moral law. In fact, in Galatians 5–6, Paul lists several of the Ten Commandments among many of the requirements for Christians in working out their sanctification.

4. **C.**

   Dr. Thomas explained that some people use the word legalism *when speaking of any sense of demand or obligation to obey God's law. This is not legalism. As Dr. Thomas explained, "It is not legalism to obey the moral law."*

5. **D.**

   The teaching that people must repent "in order to come to Christ" has sometimes been called preparationism. *It is not a biblical approach to repentance. Even though we are required to repent of our sins, we do not prepare ourselves so that Christ can receive us through repentance. That would be an improper view of the place of repentance in the Christian experience. Though God requires repentance of us, we are not justified by our repentance. We initially come to Christ by faith.*

6. **B.**

   The Apostle Paul had already told the members of the churches in Galatia: "I have been crucified with Christ. It is no longer I who live, but Christ who lives in me" (Gal. 2:20). In 4:19, he addresses them as "my little children, for whom I am again in the anguish of childbirth until Christ is formed in you!" Paul was reminding them of what God does in them through the same gospel that he had received. When Paul believed, Christ was formed in him. When they believed, Christ was formed in them. When they turned to another gospel, they lost the joy of the indwelling Christ. Paul's great longing and earnest labor was for Christ to be formed in them again through the gospel.

9

Set Free in Christ

INTRODUCTION

The letter to Galatians is the Apostle Paul's great defense of the gospel and—by implication—of the freedom that believers have in Christ. Having introduced the subject of the believer's adoption into the family of God through faith in Christ, Paul gives an allegory of Abraham's two wives and two sons. In this lesson, Dr. Thomas unfolds the mystery of the gospel allegory of Hagar and Sarah.

LEARNING GOALS

When you have finished this lesson, you should be able to:

- Explain why Paul appeals to Genesis 16 in his defense of the gospel
- Identify the role of each person in this divinely inspired allegory
- Describe the connection between the conscience, legalism, and persecution

KEY IDEAS

- God gives grace freely to the undeserving, to the broken, and to failures.
- Salvation is entirely based on the sovereign intervention of God—not by human effort, intuition, or cleverness.
- Believers must keep their consciences free from rules and laws by which God has not intended for them to have their consciences bound.

REFLECTION & DISCUSSION QUESTIONS

Before the Video

What Do You Think?

Take a moment to answer the following questions. They will prepare you for the lecture.

- To whom does God give grace?

- When you think about the recipients of God's grace, what kinds of people come to mind?

Scripture Reading

"Sing, O barren one, who did not bear; break forth into singing and cry aloud, you who have not been in labor! For the children of the desolate one will be more than the children of her who is married," says the LORD.

—Isaiah 54:1

- What does this passage teach us about the grace of God toward a spiritually barren people?

During the Video

Answer the following questions while you watch the video. They will guide you through the lecture.

Grace to the Barren   *0:00–16:44*

- What is important about Paul's theological and literary understanding of the story of Hagar and Sarah in Genesis 16?

- What does the allegory of Hagar and Sarah teach us about justification by faith alone through grace alone?

The Freedom of the Gospel   *16:44–22:28*

- How does the allegory of Hagar and Sarah relate to what was happening in Galatia?

- What is the relationship between the conscience and legalism?

After the Video

Answer the following questions after you have finished the lecture. They will help you identify and summarize the major points.

- What do we learn about God's grace in salvation from Sarah's conceiving in her old age?

  If you are in a group, have the members discuss the importance of knowing and believing that God alone can bring about salvation. Do you ever find yourself thinking, speaking, or acting as though salvation were based on your own works or efforts?

- What point did Dr. Thomas make about the use of the warning related to the Lord's Supper in 1 Corinthians 11:27–34?

  If you are in a group, have the members discuss how they have understood the warnings in 1 Corinthians 11. Consider asking questions such as these: Have you ever felt unworthy to come to the table? If you have, were you looking to your own works for your right to eat the bread and drink the wine?

- How does Paul connect persecution to legalism?

  If you are in a group, have the members discuss ways to respond to legalism—imposed from within or without—as soon as they realize that it is occurring.

PRAYER

Commit what you have learned from God's Word in this lesson to prayer.

- Praise God for sovereignly saving you according to His promise.
- Confess ways in which you have sinfully allowed your conscience to be bound by laws that God has not commanded you to observe.
- Thank God for enabling you to see that salvation is entirely by grace.
- Ask God to give you a conscience singularly bound by God's Word.

REVIEW QUIZ

Use these multiple-choice questions to measure what you learned from this lesson.

1. When should we engage in an allegorical reading of the Old Testament?
   a. Only when it would be spiritually beneficial
   b. Only when Scripture teaches us to do so
   c. Only when it relates to Christ
   d. All of the above

2. What lesson do we learn from Sarah's barrenness?
   a. Barrenness is a result of unbelief.
   b. God gives grace to the barren and desolate.
   c. God blessed Sarah for her ingenuity with Hagar.
   d. There will be an earthly end to the believer's suffering.

3. We are to approach the Lord's Supper with a sense of fear and trepidation.
   a. True
   b. False

4. What specific matter regarding liberty of conscience did Paul write about in 1 Corinthians 8 and Romans 14?
   a. Whether a believer could eat ceremonially unclean foods
   b. Whether a believer had to observe feasts and festivals
   c. Whether a believer could drink alcoholic beverages
   d. Whether a believer could eat meat offered to idols

5. What declaration did Martin Luther make regarding his conscience?
   a. It was captive to God's Word alone
   b. It was constantly in a state of guilt
   c. It was in need of being renewed every day
   d. It was enslaved to man-made rules

6. What is it when a person or organization seeks to impose on our consciences something that God's Word does not?
   a. A secondary issue
   b. An error of judgment
   c. A form of persecution
   d. A minor difference among brethren

Answer Key—Set Free in Christ

REFLECTION & DISCUSSION QUESTIONS

Before the Video

What Do You Think?

> *These are personal questions. The answers should be based on your own knowledge and experience.*

Scripture Reading

- What does this passage teach us about the grace of God toward a spiritually barren people?

   Picking up the teaching of Genesis 16 about Sarah, Isaiah follows the prophecy of the Suffering Servant in Isaiah 53 with the promise of a once-barren nation bearing spiritual children. In the same way that Paul uses the allegory of Sarah and Hagar, Isaiah is reflecting on the promise of God's grace to the barren, to the broken, and to failures. The Apostle Paul appeals to this passage to explain that God has promised to make His church fruitful by the promise of His grace.

During the Video

Grace to the Barren

- What is important about Paul's theological and literary understanding of the story of Hagar and Sarah in Genesis 16?

   In Galatians 4:21–31, the Apostle appealed to the story of Hagar and Sarah in Genesis 16 as an allegory. Though the characters in the Abraham narrative were historical figures, Paul speaks of them in a way that was similar to John Bunyan's use of characters in The Pilgrim's Progress.

- What does the allegory of Hagar and Sarah teach us about justification by faith alone through grace alone?

   Paul goes back to Genesis 16 to teach that there are two contrasting views about justification—one by the flesh and the other by faith. These two views of justification are represented by Hagar and Sarah and by Isaac and Ishmael. Sarah and Isaac represent the way of justification by faith alone through grace alone. Sarah was a free woman; Hagar was a slave. Isaac was the son of promise; Ishmael was the son of the fleshly attempt of Abraham to fulfill God's promise. Hagar and Ishmael represent ways of attempting to be justified by the flesh, while Sarah was past the age of bearing children when she conceived, and the birth of Isaac was by the free grace and promise of God.

The Freedom of the Gospel

- How does the allegory of Hagar and Sarah relate to what was happening in Galatia?

  The false teachers in the churches in Galatia were seeking to convince believers that they needed to make themselves worthy to be assured of their standing before God. By insisting on the observation of ceremonial laws of the Old Testament, the false teachers were encouraging the Galatian believers to seek justification by the flesh rather than by the free grace and promise of God. The allegory of Hagar and Sarah perfectly illustrated the way in which many seek justification before God by works rather than by grace. Paul says that these two women represented two covenants—one by grace, the other by works.

- What is the relationship between the conscience and legalism?

  In this lesson, Dr. Thomas explained, "Legalism is obeying out of conscience laws which God does not demand." If we allow our consciences to be bound by man-made rules and regulation or laws that God no longer requires His people to observe, we have fallen into legalism. There are many ways that people allow their consciences to be unbiblically bound to laws that forbid them to taste, touch, or handle. When they then fail to obey laws that God has not commanded them to obey, their consciences condemn them. Jesus died to free His people from the imposition of unbiblical laws on their consciences.

After the Video

- What do we learn about God's grace in salvation from Sarah's conceiving in her old age?

  Sarah was barren until she was ninety. She was past the age of bearing children. She was fragile and broken, having endured much heartbreak over her barrenness. The point of Paul's mentioning Sarah's barrenness in the allegory is that the gospel is for the broken and for failures. We can do nothing to bring about the desired result. Salvation is not by human effort, initiative, or intuition. Salvation is entirely the work of God's sovereign intervention. Like Sarah's conception, salvation is a miracle of God.

- What point did Dr. Thomas make about the use of the warning related to the Lord's Supper in 1 Corinthians 11:27–34?

  Something extremely wicked was repeatedly occurring during the Lord's Supper in Corinth. Paul warned the Corinthians to examine themselves as to whether they were worthily partaking of the supper. Many have misunderstood what Paul was saying when he spoke of partaking worthily, thinking that they have to be good enough to partake. Dr. Thomas told the story of John Duncan, the great Scottish pastor of the nineteenth century, urging a woman in his congregation to partake when she did not think herself worthy to partake. Duncan put the cup in her hand and said: "Take it, woman. It's for sinners." That is the point of the Lord's Supper. Jesus died for us because we are unworthy in and of ourselves—not because we are worthy.

- How does Paul connect persecution to legalism?

  In Galatians 4:29, Paul notes that Ishmael persecuted Isaac. Legalism is a form of persecution. Legalists tend to manipulate and seek to control. Just as Ishmael persecuted Isaac, so the Judaizers were exercising a form of persecution over the members of the church in Galatia by trying to steal their freedom. Whenever a legalist seeks to exercise this persecuting control, we must resist and hold fast to the freedom for which Christ has set us free.

REVIEW QUIZ

Lesson 9

1. **B.**

   We are not free to engage in an allegorical reading of the Old Testament unless Scripture itself teaches us to do so. The Apostle Paul did not regularly interpret the Old Testament in this way. There have been many abuses of allegorical readings of the Old Testament throughout the history of the church. For instance, Origen in the early church and many theologians in the medieval church taught that we should interpret all Old Testament historical narratives allegorically. If we seek to engage in our own allegorical interpretations of the Old Testament, we will often err.

2. **B.**

   Sarah's barrenness would have been a great burden to her. She was not simply barren; she was broken and fragile. There is a sense in which she was—in the history of salvation—a failure at that point because she could not raise up a child to Abraham. Sarah's barrenness teaches us that salvation is entirely of the Lord and that God gives grace to the barren and desolate.

3. **B.**

   Sometimes the warning in 1 Corinthians 11 has been used to produce a sense of fear, dread, and trepidation in those coming to the table. This is not the way that we ought to think about the Lord's Supper. Rather, we should view it as a celebration, a foretaste of the marriage supper of the Lamb. We observe the Lord's Supper in anticipation of the family meal that we will have together in glory at the end of our pilgrimage.

4. **D.**

   In both 1 Corinthians 8 and Romans 14, Paul dealt with the issue of Christians' eating meat offered to idols. Some believed that it was wrong for a Christian to eat food that had been offered to an idol. Paul taught believers that food will not condemn them (1 Cor. 8:8).

5. **A.**

Luther famously explained that his conscience was held captive to the Word of God alone. When he was asked to recant at the Diet of Worms, he said, "My conscience is captive to the Word of God; I cannot and will not recant anything, for to go against conscience is neither right nor safe." Likewise, our consciences are to be held captive only to the Word of God.

6. **C.**

Though we may have a tendency to downplay the severity of unbiblical conscience-binding, Dr. Thomas explained that it is a form of persecution. The Judaizers were persecuting Christians by their insistence on the observance of old covenant ceremonial laws. Just as Ishmael had persecuted Isaac, so the Judaizers were persecuting believers with their unbiblical laws.

10

Standing in Freedom

INTRODUCTION

In the previous section of Galatians, the Apostle Paul introduced the idea of spiritual freedom with the allegory of Hagar and Sarah. Paul then moves on to call the members of the churches in Galatia to hold fast to that freedom by setting out the several ways in which it can be lost. In this lesson, Dr. Thomas walks us through Galatians 5:1–15 to set out the various threats to the freedom that we have in Christ.

LEARNING GOALS

When you have finished this lesson, you should be able to:

- Define the nature of the freedom we have in Christ
- Identify the numerous ways by which we can lose our spiritual freedom

KEY IDEAS

- Christ has set believers free from attempts at self-justification, from trying to win God's favor, and from the burden of an unbiblically bound conscience.
- Our spiritual freedom in Christ is threatened when we take it for granted.
- Keeping our eyes on Jesus is one of the chief ways for us to preserve our freedom in Him.
- When we make our guilt or performance the measure of our justification, we jeopardize the freedom we have in Christ.
- Those who understand the freedom they have in Christ live consecrated lives of obedience to God.

REFLECTION & DISCUSSION QUESTIONS

Before the Video

What Do You Think?

> Take a moment to answer the following questions. They will prepare you for the lecture.
>
> - How often do you reflect on the blessing of having been set free in Christ?
>
> - In what ways does the freedom you have in Christ affect your daily actions and interactions?

Scripture Reading

> *You are severed from Christ, you who would be justified by the law; you have fallen away from grace.*
>
> —Galatians 5:4
>
> - What does this verse teach us about the error into which the members of the churches of Galatia had fallen?

During the Video

> Answer the following questions while you watch the video. They will guide you through the lecture.

The Threats of Legalism   *0:00–17:23*

> - Why does Paul command believers to stand fast in the freedom they have been given in Christ?
>
> - How is legalism diametrically opposed to keeping our eyes on Jesus?
>
> - How was the reception of circumcision an attempt by the Galatians to measure their justification?

The Threat of Lawlessness   *17:23–22:32*

- How is our freedom in Christ threatened by thinking that we can live as we please?

- What is wrong with thinking that God will love you only if you obey?

After the Video

Answer the following questions after you have finished the lecture. They will help you identify and summarize the major points.

- From what has Christ set believers free?

If you are in a group, have the members discuss the importance of experiencing true freedom in Christ. What effect does the loss of this freedom have on your Christian living? How often do you talk about freedom in Christ with other believers?

- How do we keep our eyes on Jesus?

If you are in a group, have the members discuss more practical ways for Christians to keep their eyes on Jesus in addition to Dr. Thomas' explanations.

- What motivates obedience in the Christian's life?

If you are in a group, have the members discuss the importance of examining what motivates our desire to obey. Consider asking questions such as these: What are some wrong motives from which we may seek to obey God? How do we know when our motives are right?

PRAYER

Commit what you have learned from God's Word in this lesson to prayer.

- Praise God for sending His Son to set you free from the bondage of sin and legalism.
- Confess ways in which you have failed to stand fast in the liberty of Christ.
- Thank God for revealing specific threats to true spiritual freedom so that you can guard against them.
- Ask God for a heart that desires to obey the Lord Jesus Christ out of a sense of gratitude for the redemption He has already provided.

REVIEW QUIZ

Use these multiple-choice questions to measure what you learned from this lesson.

1. From what do true Christians experience freedom?
    a. The burden of having to justify ourselves
    b. The burden of trying to win God's favor
    c. The burden of those who would judge us
    d. All of the above

2. How is spiritual freedom threatened?
    a. By our taking it for granted
    b. By our taking our eyes off Jesus
    c. By our measuring our justification by our performance
    d. All of the above

3. What did Peter call the ceremonial law at the Jerusalem Council in Acts 15?
    a. A gracious pattern of obedience
    b. A matter of indifference
    c. A yoke of slavery
    d. A way of life

4. In Galatians 5:4, Paul is teaching that a true believer can fall away from grace.
    a. True
    b. False

5. What happens when guilt becomes the measure of your justification?
    a. Your faith becomes the measure of your justification.
    b. Your conscience becomes the measure of your justification.
    c. Your performance becomes the measure of your justification.
    d. Your joy becomes the measure of your justification.

6. What is faith joined with in Galatians 5:6?
    a. Fear
    b. Obedience
    c. Circumcision
    d. Love

Answer Key—Standing in Freedom

Before the Video

What Do You Think?

> *These are personal questions. The answers should be based on your own knowledge and experience.*

Scripture Reading

- What does this verse teach us about the error into which the members of the churches of Galatia had fallen?

  The members of the church had allowed themselves to be deceived by the Judaizers' false gospel. They had started to believe that they could be "justified by the law." They were seeking a right standing before God on the basis of their works. In so doing, they had separated themselves from Christ. Righteousness comes only by faith in Christ. Any attempt at self-justification is futile and antithetical to the grace of God in the gospel.

During the Video

The Threats of Legalism

- Why does Paul command believers to stand fast in the freedom they have been given in Christ?

  Because professing believers can take spiritual freedom in Christ for granted, Paul opens Galatians 5 with a command to stand fast in that freedom. There is an ever-present danger of taking our freedom in Christ for granted. We are all susceptible to starting the Christian life by the Spirit and then trying to complete it in the flesh. We must resist the mind-set that tells us that we need Christ at the beginning of our Christian life but that the rest of the Christian life is up to us.

- How is legalism diametrically opposed to keeping our eyes on Jesus?

  The Galatians had deceived themselves into thinking that if they accepted circumcision, they would be more acceptable to God. They put their focus on their works and performance. We can do the same in many ways. For instance, if we start to look at external dress codes or interests or systems of value that will make us acceptable to God, we have done the same thing. What we are looking at for our acceptance before God is what matters. If we are looking at laws, obedience, or conformity to a set of standards rather than at Jesus, we have taken our eyes off Jesus and jeopardized the freedom we have in Him.

- How was the reception of circumcision an attempt by the Galatians to measure their justification?

  Circumcision was the first of many ceremonial laws in old covenant Israel. Once the Galatians bound themselves to it, they were binding themselves to perfect and continual obedience of every other law that followed. Paul summarizes this principle in Galatians 5:3, where he writes, "I testify again to every man who accepts circumcision that he is obligated to keep the whole law." In this sense, their reception of circumcision became a measurement of their justification.

The Threat of Lawlessness

- How is our freedom in Christ threatened by thinking that we can live as we please?

  Paul explains that our liberty in Christ is threatened by an antinomian approach to Christianity, living as though we could do whatever we wanted. Spiritual freedom in Christ is not only threatened by legalism, but also threatened by lawlessness. In Galatians 5:13, Paul explains: "You were called to freedom, brothers. Only do not use your freedom as an opportunity for the flesh."

- What is wrong with thinking that God will love you only if you obey?

  God has loved His people with an everlasting love. He loves His own with infinite love. We cannot secure the love of God by our obedience. We obey because He has loved us and given His Son for us. We do not obey in order to merit His love. We love Him in response to His love for us. We obey Him out of gratitude, not out of a desire to secure His love.

After the Video

- From what has Christ set believers free?

  Jesus died to liberate believers from the bondage of legalistic mind-sets and lives. Christ has set believers free from the burden of self-justification, from the burden of trying to gain God's gracious favor by our works, and from the burden of efforts to bind our consciences with man-made laws or societal values.

- How do we keep our eyes on Jesus?

  We keep our eyes on Jesus by meditating on what He has accomplished for us in His life and death. This involves reminding ourselves of Christ's perfect obedience, His sacrificial death, His resurrection, His ascension, and His return. The more we keep our mind and heart focused on the person and work of Christ, the less we will be tempted to turn our eyes on anything that would take away from what He has accomplished for us.

- What motivates obedience in the Christian's life?

  In Galatians 5:6, Paul refers to "faith working through love." Faith works through love out of gratitude for God's calling us into union and communion with Christ.

Saving faith will result in a life of obedience and the freedom of loving Christ and our neighbors: "For you were called to freedom, brothers. Only do not use your freedom as an opportunity for the flesh, but through love serve one another. For the whole law is fulfilled in one word: 'You shall love your neighbor as yourself'" (Gal. 5:13–14).

REVIEW QUIZ

Lesson 10

1. **D.**

   When Scripture says, "If the Son sets you free, you will be free indeed" (John 8:36), it is referring to the freedom that God gives us in Christ from the burden of having to justify ourselves, the burden of trying to win God's favor, and the burden of an unbiblically bound conscience.

2. **D.**

   Throughout this lesson, Dr. Thomas explained that our spiritual freedom in Christ is threatened when we take it for granted, take our eyes off Jesus, and measure our justification by our performance. The members of the churches in Galatia were in danger of doing all these things when they entertained the false gospel of the Judaizers.

3. **C.**

   In Acts 15:10, Peter asked those who insisted on the observance of the ceremonial law, "Why are you putting God to the test by placing a yoke on the neck of the disciples that neither our fathers nor we have been able to bear?" Calling others to keep the ceremonial laws in the new covenant was equivalent to placing a yoke of bondage on them. It was a form of legalism that had no limits. It called them to do more and more in order to obtain a right standing with God. It led to joyless enslavement.

4. **B.**

   When Paul wrote, "You are severed from Christ, you who would be justified by the law; you have fallen away from grace," he was not intimating that a true believer can fall away from the grace of God. Rather, he was speaking in hypothetical terms. As Dr. Thomas explained: "If this is the direction you're going, you might as well be severed from Christ because you're not looking to Him, and the measurement of your justification is now yourself. . . . You've forgotten grace. You've forgotten that salvation is a free gift."

5. **C.**

   When we allow a sense of conviction of guilt to become the measure of our justification, we inevitably start to make our performance the measure of our justification. When we do that, we are no longer trusting in Christ; rather, we are trusting in ourselves. The gospel is for sinners like David, who, though he sinned grievously with Bathsheba, trusted in God's promise rather than in his own obedience.

6. **D.**

   In Galatians 5:6, Paul makes it clear that in Christ the only thing that matters is "faith working through love." The same faith that justifies us is active in leading to a life of obedience. It is because God loved us and gave Christ for us that we can respond to His commands out of gratitude for what He has done for us.

11

Walking by the Spirit

INTRODUCTION

Shifting his attention away from his warnings about the Judaizers, the Apostle Paul turns to address the Christian's call to holiness. Galatians teaches that the Spirit of God enables Christians to live a life of obedience to the Lord out of gratitude for what He has done for us in Christ. In this lesson, Dr. Thomas covers Galatians 5:16–26 and its teaching on gospel holiness through walking by the Spirit.

LEARNING GOALS

When you have finished this lesson, you should be able to:

- Define the concept of holiness
- Explain the role that the Spirit plays in making believers holy
- Identify the specific characteristics of living by the flesh and living by the Spirit
- Recognize the reality of spiritual warfare in the Christian life

KEY IDEAS

- Personal holiness is the greatest need that a believer has in this life.
- The Holy Spirit is the agent of holiness, since He enables God's people to put sin to death.
- Christians are called to confess specific sins and pursue specific marks of holiness.
- We must be aware that we are engaged in a spiritual battle with the evil one while recognizing the constant internal conflict between the flesh and the Spirit.

REFLECTION & DISCUSSION QUESTIONS

Before the Video

What Do You Think?

Take a moment to answer the following questions. They will prepare you for the lecture.

- What is true holiness?

- Why is the pursuit of holiness such a challenging part of the Christian life?

Scripture Reading

Walk by the Spirit, and you will not gratify the desires of the flesh. For the desires of the flesh are against the Spirit, and the desires of the Spirit are against the flesh, for these are opposed to each other, to keep you from doing the things you want to do.

—Galatians 5:16–17

- What does this passage teach us about the irreconcilable war in which believers are engaged?

During the Video

Answer the following questions while you watch the video. They will guide you through the lecture.

The Root and Agent of Holiness   *0:00–12:32*

- What does holiness look like?

- What is the root of holiness?

- Who is the agent of holiness?

The Experience and Details of Holiness   *12:32–22:51*

- What conflict does a Christian experience in the pursuit of holiness?

- What two lists does Paul give us to help us understand the details of holiness?

After the Video

Answer the following questions after you have finished the lecture. They will help you identify and summarize the major points.

- How does someone become a saint?

  If you are in a group, have the members read 1 Corinthians 1:2. What does this verse tell us about the status of every believer in the church? How should this shape our view of ourselves in the church and in the world?

- What is faulty about the Keswick view of sanctification?

  If you are in a group, have the members discuss the reality of progressive sanctification in light of the inner conflict in which we are always engaged in this life. What detrimental effect does a view of perfectionism have on a Christian's inner life?

- Why is it not enough to generally ask the Lord for forgiveness of sin? Why is it important for us to confess particular sins to Him?

  If you are in a group, have the members discuss the importance of confessing specific sins on a daily basis. Consider asking questions such as these: How often do you stop throughout the day to confess your sins to the Lord? Is it your practice to reflect on the specific ways in which you have transgressed or failed to keep His law?

PRAYER

Commit what you have learned from God's Word in this lesson to prayer.

- Praise God for giving you the Holy Spirit so that you can live a life of holiness.
- Confess how you have given in to the lusts of the flesh and have failed to walk according to the Spirit.
- Thank God for renewing in you a desire to pursue a life of holiness.
- Ask God that He would cause the fruit of the Spirit to be born in your life.

REVIEW QUIZ

Use these multiple-choice questions to measure what you learned from this lesson.

1. According to Robert Murray M'Cheyne, what is the church's greatest need?
   a. Silent reflection
   b. Fervent service
   c. Passionate preaching
   d. Personal holiness

2. What is the role of the Holy Spirit?
   a. The Spirit is the inspirer of Scripture.
   b. The Spirit is the agent of regeneration.
   c. The Spirit is the One who leads believers into holiness.
   d. All of the above

3. According to Dr. Thomas, what does Paul mean when he speaks of "the evil day" (Eph. 6:13)?
   a. The day Jesus died
   b. The final era of human history
   c. The fallen course of humanity
   d. The special periods of Satan's activity

4. What does Augustine's doctrine of prevenient grace propose?
   a. That we work for our salvation
   b. That God gives everyone preparatory grace enabling each person to choose Christ
   c. That the Spirit enables us to work out what God is working in us
   d. None of the above

5. What are the marks of holiness in a Christian's life?
   a. Denying yourself certain foods and drinks
   b. Putting sin to death and putting on godliness
   c. Putting on an external demeanor of godliness
   d. All of the above

6. To what does Paul refer when he speaks of the leading of the Holy Spirit?
   a. The supernatural guidance of the Spirit
   b. The spiritual gift of discernment
   c. Spirit-produced holiness
   d. The audible voice of God

Answer Key—Walking by the Spirit

REFLECTION & DISCUSSION QUESTIONS

Before the Video

What Do You Think?

These are personal questions. The answers should be based on your own knowledge and experience.

Scripture Reading

- What does this passage teach us about the irreconcilable war in which believers are engaged?

  The Apostle Paul teaches us that the flesh and the Spirit are diametrically opposed. The believer has an ongoing conflict because of the indwelling of the Spirit wrestling against sinful desires. The Holy Spirit enables believers to grow in holiness by helping them deny the desires of the flesh. However, the flesh is ever present, urging us to do what is displeasing to God.

During the Video

The Root and Agent of Holiness

- What does holiness look like?

  Holiness looks like Christlikeness. Jesus is the embodiment of holiness. In union with Christ, we are made more like Christ by the work of the Holy Spirit. As Dr. Thomas explained, "Holiness is the reproduction of the character of Jesus within us so that we might reflect what Jesus is like."

- What is the root of holiness?

  There is a twofold root of holiness for believers. First, there is the Christian's union with Christ. We see this in the words "those who belong to Christ Jesus" in Galatians 5:24. God has redeemed us so that we would be in union and fellowship with Christ: "You are in Christ Jesus, who became to us . . . sanctification" (1 Cor. 1:30). The other root of holiness is our being crucified with Christ. Our old man was crucified with Christ so that we might live in newness of life in union with Him.

- Who is the agent of holiness?

  The Holy Spirit is the agent of our holiness. The third person of the Godhead is the only member of the Trinity who bears the descriptor "holy" because He is the agent of our sanctification. Though we are called to form holy habits and put sin to death, we can do so only by the Holy Spirit at work within us. We are to work out what God is working in us by the Holy Spirit.

The Experience and Details of Holiness

- What conflict does a Christian experience in the pursuit of holiness?

  Every Christian is conflicted because every Christian wants to serve and obey God; however, we still do the things we don't want to do and we fail to do the things we want to do. This is the teaching of the Apostle Paul in Galatians 5:17 and Romans 7. We live in a constant struggle with Satan and our own flesh. We are fighting not to take our eyes off Jesus and not to give in to the sinful desires of the flesh. We are called to put sin to death, and there are times and seasons when we are in deep spiritual conflict and warfare.

- What two lists does Paul give us to help us understand the details of holiness?

  In Galatians 5:19–23, the Apostle gives us two lists to help us see the details of holiness—a vice list and a grace list. The vice list consists of the specific sins that accord with our fleshly desires: "sexual immorality, impurity, sensuality, idolatry, sorcery, enmity, strife, jealousy, fits of anger, rivalries, dissensions, divisions, envy, drunkenness, orgies, and things like these" (vv. 19–21). The grace list comprises the various aspects of the fruit of the Spirit—"love, joy, peace, patience, kindness, goodness, faithfulness, gentleness, self-control" (vv. 22–23).

After the Video

- How does someone become a saint?

  The Apostle Paul opens his letter to the church in Corinth by addressing the members of the church as "saints." Contrary to the teaching of the Roman Catholic Church, you do not have to perform a single miracle in order to attain the status of a saint. Because believers are definitively sanctified in Christ, every believer is a saint. We are no longer what we were. We are saints and holy ones because of our union with Christ. That is our new identity.

- What is faulty about the Keswick view of sanctification?

  The Keswick school of theology taught the faulty belief that an individual could attain a stage of sanctification in this life in which the soul is quiet and the war is finished. This was also John Wesley's view of perfectionism in the Christian life. Such notions go against the teaching and experience of the Apostle Paul. In Galatians 5 and Romans 7, Paul taught about the ongoing warfare in the life of believers. Paul explained that he was in conflict in his inner man.

- Why is it not enough to generally ask the Lord for forgiveness of sin? Why is it important for us to confess particular sins to Him?

  In the list of vices in Galatians 5:19–21, Paul details specific sins. This teaches us the importance of acknowledging our sins in specific ways. Since sins have specific names, we should name our sins accordingly when we confess them to the Lord. Doing so is also a means of putting specific sins to death in our lives. The more we confess specific sins to God, the more we will be conscious of our need to fight against those specific sins.

REVIEW QUIZ

Lesson 11

1. **D.**

   The Scottish pastor Robert Murray M'Cheyne once stated that the greatest need of his church was his personal holiness. Likewise, the greatest need of all believers is personal holiness. We need personal holiness so that we reflect to others that we are truly living for Christ. True holiness is being conformed to the image of Christ.

2. **D.**

   The Holy Spirit fills many roles. For instance, He is the inspirer of Scripture. The Spirit worked in the authors of Scripture to produce the written Word of God. The Spirit also gives new life to God's people, bringing them from spiritual death to spiritual life through regeneration. Finally, the Spirit—as His name indicates—produces holiness in the lives of those He has regenerated. The Holy Spirit is principally concerned with holiness.

3. **D.**

   In the lesson, Dr. Thomas explained that Paul's reference to "the evil day" is shorthand for "days when Satan is particularly busy." There are times in the Christian's life when Satan, or one of his workers, is seeking to cause as much of a mess as possible. This is part of the conflict in which the believer is engaged in this life. Because we live in this war zone, Paul charges Christians to take up the armor of God.

4. **C.**

   Augustine's doctrine of prevenient grace teaches that the Spirit works in us to enable us to cooperate in our pursuit of holiness. We work out what God is working in us (Phil. 2:12–13). The Spirit is the agent of our sanctification. We cannot do anything without the working of the Spirit in our hearts.

5. **B.**

   In Colossians 3:5–17, the Apostle Paul gives two lists of those actions that those who are in union with Jesus Christ should put off and put on. True holiness is a work of the Holy Spirit that is also marked by actions on our part. Some of these are habit-forming actions that take the shape of holiness. The marks of holiness are demonstrated in our putting sin to death and putting on righteousness.

6. **C.**

   When Paul wrote, "If you are led by the Spirit, you are not under the law" (Gal. 5:18), he was referring to the way in which the Spirit of God leads the believer into paths of holiness. He was not speaking in terms of personal guidance for decision-making. The Spirit, as the agent of the sanctification of God's people, leads the believer into Christlikeness.

12

Gracious Restoration

INTRODUCTION

After setting out the works of the flesh and the fruit of the Spirit, Paul introduces a series of gospel applications to address interpersonal relationships in the churches of Galatia. He teaches that a right view of justification will necessarily affect how we interact with one another. In this lesson, Dr. Thomas examines Paul's call to gospel obedience in bearing the burdens of our brothers and sisters in Christ.

LEARNING GOALS

When you have finished this lesson, you should be able to:

- Explain the erroneous views of self that we adopt when we are not focused on the gospel
- Recognize the way in which the gospel shapes our desire to care for the needs and bear the burdens of others

KEY IDEAS

- We have forgotten our identity in Christ when we have too high or too low a view of ourselves.
- If we live with a mind-set of superiority or inferiority toward fellow Christians, we will provoke and envy one another.
- We should be quick to forgive, restore, and cover the offenses of our brothers and sisters in Christ, since we have all been forgiven by God in Christ.

REFLECTION & DISCUSSION QUESTIONS

Before the Video

What Do You Think?

Take a moment to answer the following questions. They will prepare you for the lecture.

- How ought we to approach other believers when we see sin in their lives? What is our obligation to our brothers and sisters in Christ?

- How should you view yourself in relation to other believers? What self-conception is commensurate with the gospel?

Scripture Reading

Bear one another's burdens, and so fulfill the law of Christ.

—Galatians 6:2

- In what way is Paul answering the legalism of the Judaizers?

During the Video

Answer the following questions while you watch the video. They will guide you through the lecture.

A Right View of Yourself   *0:00–8:20*

- In Galatians 5:26, who are the two types of people with a wrong view of self?

- What is the result of these two wrong views of self?

- What is the solution to a wrong view of self?

A Right View of Others   *8:20–22:37*

- According to Galatians 6:1, what kind of person will have a right view of others?

- How should we approach a brother or sister in need of spiritual restoration?

- How should we approach someone in love when that person sins against us?

After the Video

Answer the following questions after you have finished the lecture. They will help you identify and summarize the major points.

- In Galatians 5:26, Paul uses a Greek word that English Bible versions have translated "conceited." According to Dr. Thomas, what is the original meaning of the word?

  If you are in a group, have the members discuss the concept of honorable behavior. Do you tend to think of conceit as dishonorable behavior? Or do you limit dishonorable behavior to scandalous sins?

- Dr. Thomas set out a number of default responses to difficult situations of those with too high or too low a view of themselves. What are they?

  If you are in a group, have the members discuss their own default responses to situations. Which of these two lists best describes your default reactions? When you are rooted in who you are in Christ, how do you respond to difficult situations and people?

- What is the connection between a wrong view of self and the doctrine of justification by faith alone?

  If you are in a group, have the members discuss our need to continually remember that God has justified us through faith alone. How are you viewing yourself when you forget that your justification before God is through faith alone in Christ alone?

PRAYER

Commit what you have learned from God's Word in this lesson to prayer.

- Praise God for forgiving your sins.
- Confess ways in which you have provoked or envied other Christians.
- Thank God for reminding you of who you are in Christ.
- Ask God to make you quick to forgive and bear the burdens of other believers.

REVIEW QUIZ

Use these multiple-choice questions to measure what you learned from this lesson.

1. When can we be at peace with ourselves?
    a. When we have done our best
    b. When we have adopted the lowest possible view of ourselves
    c. When we have a high self-esteem
    d. When we know who we are in Christ

2. Dr. Thomas named two extremes in Galatians. What are they?
    a. Moralism and antinomianism
    b. Hedonism and moralism
    c. Pacifism and legalism
    d. Anarchism and moralism

3. Dr. Thomas mentioned a hymn commonly attributed to John Calvin. Which attribute of Christ does this hymn focus on?
    a. The righteousness of Christ
    b. The gentleness of Christ
    c. The justice of Christ
    d. The power of Christ

4. What should your goal be in pursuing someone in the manner of Matthew 18?
    a. To make a public example of the person
    b. To let the person know that you are spiritual
    c. To remove the person from the fellowship
    d. To resolve an offense with an aim at restoration

5. What is one of the foremost characteristics of love in regard to sin?
    a. Love shines a judgmental light on a multitude of sins
    b. Love is apathetic about a multitude of sins
    c. Love shames a multitude of sins
    d. Love covers a multitude of sins

6. What are we to do with the burdens of fellow Christians?
    a. Make them a public example for the sake of others
    b. Overlook them to help those with burdens produce patience
    c. Bear them and so fulfill the law of Christ
    d. Heap on requirements to build character

Answer Key—Gracious Restoration

Before the Video

What Do You Think?

> *These are personal questions. The answers should be based on your own knowledge and experience.*

Scripture Reading

- In what way is Paul answering the legalism of the Judaizers?

> *The Judaizers were placing legalistic burdens on the members of the Galatian churches by insisting that they observe the ceremonial law of Moses. This was bringing the Galatians into bondage. The result was that they were no longer living as those in union with Christ. As Paul turned his attention to the issue of gospel obedience, he explained that those who abide in Christ will be a people who bear the burdens of one another. They will seek to carry the heavy load rather than place it on someone else. By so doing, they will find that love—and not works-righteousness—is actually the fulfillment of the law.*

During the Video

A Right View of Yourself

- In Galatians 5:26, who are the two types of people with a wrong view of self?

> *When Paul says, "Let us not become conceited, provoking one another, envying one another," he has two types of people in mind—those who think that they are superior to others and those who think that they are inferior. The first group comprises people who believe that they are better than others because of their gift, talents, or providences. Those in the second group think that they are inferior to others because they are fundamentally unsure about themselves.*

- What is the result of these two wrong views of self?

> *When we have a faulty view of ourselves, we fall into one of two errors. Those who believe they are superior to others have a tendency to provoke others, and those who believe they are inferior have a propensity to envy others. Both these errors stem from a works-based mentality and result in our thinking of ourselves more highly or more lowly than we ought to.*

- What is the solution to a wrong view of self?

> *We will have a right view of self only when we remember the gospel. We need to be settled with who we are in Christ. We have peace of mind when we remember that*

Christ has redeemed us. We need to remember that we have been crucified with Christ, united to Christ, forgiven in Christ, and adopted into God's family through Christ. When we remember our identity in Christ, we will not try to find our identity in our gifts or compare ourselves with others.

A Right View of Others

- According to Galatians 6:1, what kind of person will have a right view of others?

  As Paul addressed the members of the church regarding the responsibility they have toward one another, he wrote, "Brothers, if anyone is caught in any transgression, you who are spiritual should restore him in a spirit of gentleness." Only spiritually minded people are able to truly care for others. Paul is insisting that only those who are indwelt by the Spirit of God can have a right view of self and therefore have a right view of others. Since we are no longer in Adam, we are called to live in light of our union with Christ. If we are led by the Spirit, we will care for the needs of others in the body.

- How should we approach a brother or sister in need of spiritual restoration?

  In Galatians 6:1, Paul charges the Galatians to restore one another "in a spirit of gentleness." Gentleness is one of the foremost characteristics of Jesus. In the Gospels, Christ appeals to this attribute: "Come to me, all who labor and are heavy laden, and I will give you rest. Take my yoke upon you, and learn from me, for I am gentle and lowly in heart, and you will find rest for your souls" (Matt. 11:28–29). Our lives are also to be marked by a spirit of gentleness.

- How should we approach someone in love when that person sins against us?

  Jesus calls us to first approach a Christian who has sinned against us in a manner consistent with Matthew 18: "If your brother sins against you, go and tell him his fault, between you and him alone" (v. 15). We are not to gossip about or avoid anyone when this happens. We should remember that "love covers a multitude of sins" (1 Peter 4:8) and approach a brother or sister in Christ with a heart that is ready to cover and restore.

After the Video

- In Galatians 5:26, Paul uses a Greek word that English Bible versions have translated "conceited." According to Dr. Thomas, what is the original meaning of the word?

  The Greek word kenodoxos means "empty of honor." Those who were acting conceited in the Galatian churches—by thinking of themselves either as superior or inferior—were acting dishonorably among themselves. Whenever we act in a way that reflects one of these two mind-sets, it will inevitably result in our provoking or envying one another. Paul drives this point home when he says, "Let us not become conceited."

- Dr. Thomas set out a number of default responses to difficult situations of those with too high or too low a view of themselves. What are they?

  Those who have a mentality of superiority tend to scream at others, start arguments, and get angry and judgmental. Those who have an inferiority complex often clam up, retreat into themselves, and make excuses. While these reactions are polar opposites, they are all outward manifestations of a misunderstanding of the gospel. As believers, we are able to rest peacefully in our identity in Christ, and our responses to others will not reflect a superiority or inferiority complex.

- What is the connection between a wrong view of self and the doctrine of justification by faith alone?

  When people find their sense of value and self-worth in their attempts to keep the law or in their own perceived obedience, they live in pride, and they begin to compare themselves with others. In turn, such individuals love to fixate on the sins of others to make themselves look better, or they fixate on another's accomplishments, believing they can never add up. When individuals fall into such errors, they have forgotten the gospel. They have a forgotten that justification is by faith alone.

REVIEW QUIZ

Lesson 12

1. **D.**

   Only when we know who we are in Christ can we be comfortable with ourselves and have peace with others. When we remember that we have been redeemed by Christ, are united to Him, and have been adopted into the family of God, we will think properly about ourselves. We will not compare ourselves to others in the body. We will not treat others with contempt or envy them.

2. **B.**

   Dr. Thomas explained that moralism and hedonism are the two extremes that Paul addresses throughout this letter. Moralism is seeking approval from God and men by law-keeping. Hedonism is rejecting rule-keeping and causing others great harm in the process. A wrong view of self is bound up in both these errors. The moralist has a superiority complex. The hedonist has an inferiority complex.

3. **B.**

   The hymn "I Greet Thee, Who My Sure Redeemer Art" focuses on the gentleness of Christ. Though Jesus was strong, there was an observable gentleness about Him. When we spend time in the presence of Christ, we can take note of this quality. Gentleness is a fruit of the Spirit of Christ Himself.

4. **D.**

   In His instructions in Matthew 18, Jesus teaches us to bring up the way we have been sinned against personally and privately. Only if we are not heard should we take two or three witnesses with us, and if this fails, we are to seek restoration through the church. Throughout this process, we should assume a spirit of gentleness, hoping for repentance and restoration.

5. **D.**

While Christ commands us to follow His directions in Matthew 18, in seeking to restore someone, there are times when we should cover sin in love. In 1 Peter 4:8, we read, "Above all, keep loving one another earnestly, since love covers a multitude of sins." Love doesn't shine a light on every sin of everyone in the church. As Dr. Thomas explained: "If we went after every sin of others, we would have nothing else to do. It would occupy us day and night." God calls believers to overlook a multitude of the brethren's transgressions.

6. **C.**

In Galatians 6:2, Paul commands the Galatians to "bear one another's burdens." We are to be people who come alongside our brothers and sisters when we see them burdened. We are not to accuse or condemn them. We are not to point out sin in others because of our own conceit. Rather, we are to be quick to pull up and help a struggling or burdened believer.

13

Stewards of Grace

INTRODUCTION

As Paul draws near to the close of his letter, he continues giving the Galatians a series of applications rooted in the gospel. In this brief section, Paul introduces the subject of gospel stewardship, explaining the important principle of reaping and sowing. In this lesson, Dr. Thomas examines the ways that Paul teaches us to be gospel stewards of our goods, bodies, and opportunities.

LEARNING GOALS

When you have finished this lesson, you should be able to:

- Explain the reason why the church should support its ministers
- Give examples of the principle of reaping and sowing

KEY IDEAS

- The way you respond in any given situation reflects your understanding of the gospel.
- Congregations have a responsibility to take care of the material needs of their teachers.
- The principle of reaping and sowing is beneficial to believers' understanding of how they ought to steward their bodies.
- We have a responsibility to be good stewards of our opportunities to do good— first of all to the household of faith and then to all those around us.

REFLECTION & DISCUSSION QUESTIONS

Before the Video

What Do You Think?

Take a moment to answer the following questions. They will prepare you for the lecture.

- Why does a congregation have a responsibility to provide for the needs of its minister?

- Whom are we responsible to care for as Christians?

Scripture Reading

Let the one who is taught the word share all good things with the one who teaches. Do not be deceived: God is not mocked, for whatever one sows, that will he also reap. For the one who sows to his own flesh will from the flesh reap corruption, but the one who sows to the Spirit will from the Spirit reap eternal life. And let us not grow weary of doing good, for in due season we will reap, if we do not give up. So then, as we have opportunity, let us do good to everyone, and especially to those who are of the household of faith.

—Galatians 6:6–10

- Why does the Apostle Paul introduce the principle of reaping and sowing in connection with our relationships with others?

During the Video

Answer the following questions while you watch the video. They will guide you through the lecture.

The Stewardship of Our Goods   *0:00–7:49*

- What were the "good things" that the Galatians were to share with their teachers?

- What is our stewardship a mark of in Paul's theology?

The Stewardship of Our Bodies and Opportunities   *7:49–22:47*

- What does Paul mean by "whatever one sows, that will he also reap"?

- What should we value above all when seeking to be stewards of our bodies? What will we reap if we sow to this most important part of our lives?

- How are we to prioritize whom we care for as good stewards of the opportunities before us?

After the Video

Answer the following questions after you have finished the lecture. They will help you identify and summarize the major points.

- According to the book of Acts, members of the early Christian community sold their possessions and had everything in common. Should that be a normative practice for us today?

  If you are in a group, have the members discuss ways in which we can be generous with our possessions in the church today. Do you pray about and plan ways that you can wisely steward what God has given you to help those in need around you?

- If the principle of reaping and sowing is biblical, why must we not conclude that when others have hardship in their lives, it is because they have sown to the flesh?

  If you are in a group, have the members read John 9:1–7. What do these verses teach about God's purpose for the blindness of the man Jesus healed? What comfort can we derive from this?

- Why is it important that Paul brought this section to a close by reminding his hearers that they ought not to "grow weary of doing good"?

  If you are in a group, have the members discuss times when they have experienced seasons of weariness. What did you do when you realized that you were in such a season? What would have happened if you had walked away from the faith or from obedience to the Lord when you felt weary?

PRAYER

Commit what you have learned from God's Word in this lesson to prayer.

- Praise God for all that He has given you in Christ.
- Confess ways that you have failed to steward your money, body, and opportunities as unto the Lord.

- Thank God for the provisions of life and for giving you the privilege of stewarding what belongs to Him.
- Ask God to open your eyes to see ways that you can grow as a faithful steward of what He has given you.

REVIEW QUIZ

Use these multiple-choice questions to measure what you learned from this lesson.

1. What does the word "share" in Galatians 6:6 mean?
   a. "To give everything away"
   b. "To divide a portion"
   c. "To have in common"
   d. "To fellowship with"

2. Whom does Paul have in mind when he commands joyful giving in the church?
   a. The wealthy members of the churches
   b. Spiritually minded members of the churches
   c. Every member of the churches
   d. The Apostolic circle

3. "You reap what you sow" is a universal principle.
   a. True
   b. False

4. What does the principle "whatever one sows, that will he also reap" teach?
   a. That for every action there is an equal and opposite reaction
   b. That our ultimate salvation is based on what we do
   c. That there are consequences to our actions
   d. That all suffering is a result of sin

5. What is the church to be in its community?
   a. Separate
   b. Salt and light
   c. Disengaged
   d. Indistinguishable

6. As the church progressed in its early days, who was primarily responsible to oversee the care of the household of faith?
   a. The wealthy members of the church
   b. All the members of the church
   c. The women of the church
   d. The deacons of the church

Answer Key—Stewards of Grace

Before the Video

What Do You Think?

These are personal questions. The answers should be based on your own knowledge and experience.

Scripture Reading

- Why does the Apostle Paul introduce the principle of reaping and sowing in connection with our relationships with others?

  We are called to be good stewards of the things that God has given us, especially toward those in the household of faith. We are to support those who labor in God's Word for us. If we are able to do good to those in need in the church or in our community, we are to be zealous to steward these opportunities as best as we can. The principle of reaping and sowing reminds those who may grow weary of doing good that, in the end, they will reap eternal life.

During the Video

The Stewardship of Our Goods

- What were the "good things" that the Galatians were to share with their teachers?

  Since the early churches almost certainly did not have a full-time minister to teach and preach God's Word to them, Paul charges the members of this church to start the practice of sharing of their goods with those who visited them to teach them. They were to share their money, their food, and perhaps even their lodging. This was a gospel principle of ministerial support. The members of the church were to learn to share their goods and possessions with a minister who taught them God's Word, so that the minister and his family would have the provisions they needed.

- What is our stewardship a mark of in Paul's theology?

  Paul understands that our stewardship is a mark of our discipleship. It communicates that we are actually disciples. Paul sees it as a natural consequence of the gospel. We have received all things from God in the gospel. Therefore, we respond by sharing what belongs to us with others. Our stewardship should reflect God's own generosity.

The Stewardship of Our Bodies and Opportunities

- What does Paul mean by "whatever one sows, that will he also reap"?

  This means that what we do has consequences. In the context of the letter, Paul is calling us to be stewards of our bodies. This is because our stewardship ultimately affects our relationships, and if we sow to the sinful desires of our flesh, we will reap corruption. If we sow pornography, we will reap a distorted view of sex. If we sow a distorted view of sex, we will reap a distorted view of other people, the gospel, and Jesus Himself. If we sow to ambition, it will reap all the fallout of burning others to get to the top. So God calls us to be stewards of our bodies.

- What should we value above all when seeking to be stewards of our bodies? What will we reap if we sow to this most important part of our lives?

  We should value our new identity in Christ and His Spirit's dwelling in us. We are new creatures in Christ, having died with Him and having been raised with Him. Our old Adamic nature died when Christ died. We were once slaves, but now we are sons of God. We have been set free by the Holy Spirit. In this life, we are sojourners heading to the new Jerusalem and are spiritual beings who are indwelt by the Holy Spirit to bear witness to the glory of Jesus. When we sow to the truth of Jesus' indwelling us by the Holy Spirit, we will reap eternal life.

- How are we to prioritize whom we care for as good stewards of the opportunities before us?

  In Galatians 6:10, Paul writes, "As we have opportunity, let us do good to everyone, and especially to those who are of the household of faith." Our responsibility to do good as we have opportunity begins with the household of faith. However, it does not stop there. We are called to do good to all. This means that whenever we have opportunity around us, we are to seek to be a blessing and to benefit the community in which God has placed us.

After the Video

- According to the book of Acts, members of the early Christian community sold their possessions and had everything in common. Should that be a normative practice for us today?

  Many have mistakenly sought to use this passage to defend the political philosophy of communism. However, this wasn't an example of government-coerced distribution of property. Rather, the historical setting of the early Christians necessitated that they care for one another in exceptional ways. The persecution they endured at the hands of unbelieving Jews often resulted in their losing businesses and possessions. The members of the fledgling church therefore needed to care for one another in this time of extraordinary need. This situation was unique to the context of the early church.

- If the principle of reaping and sowing is biblical, why must we not conclude that when others have hardship in their lives, it is because they have sown to the flesh?

  Dr. Thomas explained that there are situations and experiences in life that do not happen to someone because the person has sinned. For instance, there is the example of Job. Job's friends concluded that his severe suffering was due to personal sin. They were wrong to draw that conclusion. Then there is the man who was born blind in John 9. The disciples asked Jesus, "Who sinned, this man or his parents, that he was born blind?" (v. 2). Jesus essentially responded, "Neither." This man wasn't suffering because of anything that he or his parents had done wrong. We must be slow to conclude that others are suffering because they have reaped to their flesh.

- Why is it important that Paul brought this section to a close by reminding his hearers that they ought not to "grow weary of doing good"?

  We feel weary in many difficult and trying seasons of life. Paul is recognizing the ever-present danger of believers' growing weary of doing good. He is reminding the people of God that they should not get weary of the Christian life. He wants us to be awake to the possibility that we will get weary so that we might guard against wanting to give up.

REVIEW QUIZ

Lesson 13

1. **C.**

   The word that Paul uses in Galatians 6:6 is the New Testament word koinōnia, which means "having in common." When Paul tells the members of the Galatians to share all good things with those who have taught them the Word of God, he is expressing his desire to see them support the itinerant ministers who were teaching them the Word of God. The New Testament churches wouldn't have organized church government beyond the Apostles for twenty to thirty more years. It was important that the congregation open their homes and share their possessions with the ministers who were visiting with them during this period.

2. **C.**

   When Paul speaks of the joy of giving and sharing, he has every member of the church in mind. He does not simply have the wealthy members in mind. Giving is a mark of discipleship. It is a principle for all professing believers. Giving is a consequence of the gospel. Since God has given us every good thing in the gospel, we are to be giving and sharing people. We are called by God to give according to our means and ability for the support and promotion of the ministry of the gospel.

3. **B.**

   While Galatians 6:7 teaches the truth that "whatever one sows, that will he also reap," the converse is not also a universal principle. We cannot say that whatever a person reaps, he has sown. This is clear from the example of the suffering of Job and the affliction of the man who was born blind (John 9). When Jesus says regarding the man born blind, "It was not that this man sinned, or his parents," He is not denying original or personal sin. However, He is teaching that affliction and hardship are not always the result of personal sin.

4. **C.**

   When Paul says, "Whatever one sows, that will he also reap," he is referring to the principle that our actions have consequences. Parents teach their children this general principle when they tell them not to run across the road. The parents explain that if the children do run across the road, they could get hit by a car. We also know this to be true of sin and its consequences in this life. This principle is true of all the ways that we may sow to our fleshly desires. There will be consequences commensurate with the nature of the sin, but not all suffering is a result of sin.

5. **B.**

   The church is to be salt and light in the community. When Paul says that we are to do good to all as we have opportunity, he is including our community. A church can be salt and light in a community in a number of ways. It can provide direct help and service in the community, or it can partner with parachurch organizations that are better equipped to minister to specific needs, such as to the homeless.

6. **D.**

   God's call to do good starts in the "household of faith." As the church progressed from its infancy, the office of deacon was established to oversee and encourage the members of the church in their generosity toward fellow members. Among the duties of deacons was caring for those in need—particularly in periods of financial need.

14

Boasting in the Cross

INTRODUCTION

As he brings his letter to the church in Galatia to a close, Paul focuses his attention on the central message of the gospel, namely, the cross of Christ. Paul defends the central importance of what Christ accomplished for the Galatians on the cross, and he does so to protect them from the Judaizers who were seeking to lead them astray. In this final lesson, Dr. Thomas considers the abiding significance of the message of the cross and how it is the Christian's only ground for boasting.

LEARNING GOALS

When you have finished this lesson, you should be able to:

- Explain the reason why Paul refers to boasting in Galatians 6:11–18
- Recognize in what way the message of the cross is central to the gospel
- Define the key concepts related to what Jesus accomplished on the cross
- Understand how the cross divides the world and the believer

KEY IDEAS

- The Judaizers were boasting in the number of converts they drew to themselves through their fleshly message of circumcision.
- In contrast to the Judaizers' boasting, Paul boasted only in the cross of Christ.
- In His death on the cross, Jesus redeemed us from our sin, propitiated the wrath of God, and reconciled us to God.
- The cross stands between the world and the Christian, making the world appear empty to Christians and making Christians appear foolish to the world.
- God has blessed us in Christ because He was cursed in our place.

REFLECTION & DISCUSSION QUESTIONS

Before the Video

What Do You Think?

Take a moment to answer the following questions. They will prepare you for the lecture.

- What do you most frequently boast about? What does your boasting reveal?

- When you think about the cross, what things come to mind? How is the cross central to the gospel?

Scripture Reading

But far be it from me to boast except in the cross of our Lord Jesus Christ, by which the world has been crucified to me, and I to the world. For neither circumcision counts for anything, nor uncircumcision, but a new creation.

—Galatians 6:14–15

- What is the double crucifixion to which Paul refers in this passage?

During the Video

Answer the following questions while you watch the video. They will guide you through the lecture.

A Reason to Boast   *0:00–5:00*

- How does Paul introduce the subject of boasting? Why does he address this subject?

- In what statement does Paul summarize and bring to a close everything in this letter?

- Why would Paul's statement about boasting in the cross have sounded strange to a first-century reader?

The Meaning of the Cross   *5:00–19:34*

- How was the cross the climax of Jesus' obedience?

- What words does Paul use to explain what Jesus accomplished on the cross? What does each of them mean?

A Farewell Blessing   *19:34–22:31*

- How is the closing benediction a sign of the gospel?

After the Video

Answer the following questions after you have finished the lecture. They will help you identify and summarize the major points.

- How does baptism convey the idea of the judgment and curse of God? In what way does baptism symbolize what Jesus did on the cross?

  If you are in a group, have the members read Luke 12:50 and 1 Corinthians 10:1–2. Talk about the relationship between judgment and salvation as it is represented in baptism and fulfilled on the cross.

- What does Paul mean when he says, "The world has been crucified to me"?

  If you are in a group, have the members read 1 John 2:15–17. How does the teaching of this passage correspond to what Paul writes in Galatians 6:14? What are some ways that we may fail to model what Paul teaches above?

- How should you respond to the benediction at the end of a worship service?

  If you are in a group, have the members discuss the importance of benedictions in a worship service. Consider asking questions such as these: Have you ever been a part of a church in which a benediction is regularly pronounced at the end of the service? What thoughts did you have about the benediction the first time you heard it in a worship service?

PRAYER

Commit what you have learned from God's Word in this lesson to prayer.

- Praise God for revealing to you the surpassing value of the message of the cross.
- Confess times that you have boasted in things other than Christ crucified.
- Thank God for showing you the emptiness of the world in light of the cross.
- Ask God to enable you to receive, remember, and remain steadfast in the gospel.

REVIEW QUIZ

Use these multiple-choice questions to measure what you learned from this lesson.

1. What was the crucifixion a symbol of to the Jews?
   a. Roman redemption
   b. Roman domination
   c. Jewish justice
   d. God's abandonment

2. What does the word *propitiation* mean?
   a. To pay the price of release
   b. To bring together two parties
   c. To appease the wrath of God
   d. To remove someone's sins

3. In the context of Galatians, what did Paul specifically have in mind when he said, "The world has been crucified to me"?
   a. The world's art and music
   b. The world's food and clothing
   c. The world's applause and approval
   d. The world's natural blessings

4. According to Dr. Thomas, what is baptism a picture of in 1 Corinthians 10?
   a. Burial with Christ
   b. The sealing of God's promises
   c. The inward reality of regeneration
   d. The judgment and curse of God

5. How did the world view Paul?
   a. As one of the greatest minds of Judaism
   b. As one of the most sacrificial humanitarians of the day
   c. As an articulate orator
   d. As a fool

6. What is a benediction?
   a. A prayer for the Spirit's presence
   b. A pronouncement of divine blessing
   c. A prayer for the needs of the church
   d. A call for the church to worship

Answer Key—Boasting in the Cross

REFLECTION & DISCUSSION QUESTIONS

Before the Video

What Do You Think?

> *These are personal questions. The answers should be based on your own knowledge and experience.*

Scripture Reading

- What is the double crucifixion to which Paul refers in this passage?

  When Paul says, "The world has been crucified to me, and I to the world," he is envisioning a double crucifixion. On the one hand, in the death of Christ, the world has nothing left to offer Paul. He is speaking in terms of what he gains or profits from the world. On the other hand, he says that because of what has happened to him in the death of Christ, he has been crucified to the world. Just as the world has nothing for Paul, Paul is a fool in the sight of the world and its values.

During the Video

A Reason to Boast

- How does Paul introduce the subject of boasting? Why does he address this subject?

  The Judaizers—who had come into the church with a false gospel—were boasting about the number of converts that they made. In Galatians 6:13, Paul says, "They desire to have you circumcised that they may boast in your flesh." Pride and a desire to one-up the Apostle motivated the Judaizers. They wanted to brag about how many of the Christian converts they had convinced to submit to circumcision. This is the background of the Apostle's declaration about his boasting only in the cross.

- In what statement does Paul summarize and bring to a close everything in this letter?

  In Galatians 6:14, Paul writes, "Far be it from me to boast except in the cross of our Lord Jesus Christ." All that we have and all that we are in Christ are summarized in this statement. The cross of Christ is the Christian's only identity. Christ crucified is the central message of the gospel. It is by the cross that we are justified and reconciled to God.

- Why would Paul's statement about boasting in the cross have sounded strange to a first-century reader?

In the first century, the cross was a symbol of Roman execution. It was an instrument of state punishment. Much like the gas chamber or a syringe used to execute a criminal today, the cross was the symbol of the death penalty in Paul's day. This would have made Paul's statement about boasting in the cross sound foolish to the unbelieving world of his day. The cross became something the world mocked because Christians held it up as the symbol of their message. First-century Roman artwork reveals the way that unbelievers mocked the early Christians for pointing to the cross as the symbol of their faith.

The Meaning of the Cross

- How was the cross the climax of Jesus' obedience?

  The whole life of Christ was a life of obedience. Throughout his ministry, Jesus told His disciples that He had to go to Jerusalem, suffer many things, be crucified, and be raised on the third day. Jesus, though Lord of all, came for this purpose. In His wilderness temptations and even through the Apostle Peter, Satan tried to stop Him from being exalted through suffering, but Jesus set Himself steadfastly to finish the work of redemption at the cross.

- What words does Paul use to explain what Jesus accomplished on the cross? What does each of them mean?

  Throughout his letters, Paul uses words like redemption, propitiation, *and* reconciliation *to explain what occurred on the cross. The word* redemption *carries with it the idea of a marketplace transaction. It was used in the first century to denote a payment to secure the release of a slave. Spiritually, we are redeemed by the cross, and it set us free from the bondage we were in to sin and self. The word* propitiation *has in view the wrath of God coming down on Jesus as our substitute. Jesus turned away the wrath of God by His death on the cross. The word* reconciliation *represents the idea of restoring broken relationships. Jesus reconciles us to God by restoring what was broken by our sin and rebellion.*

A Farewell Blessing

- How is the closing benediction a sign of the gospel?

  A benediction is a statement of blessing that God pronounces over His people through a minister at the end of a worship service. Benedictions are rooted in the truth of the gospel. Jesus was cursed on the cross that we might be blessed by God. The specific benediction that the Apostle Paul pronounced over the Galatians is full of gospel significance. In Galatians 6:18, he declared: "The grace of our Lord Jesus Christ be with your spirit, brothers. Amen" The benediction is a reminder to Christians that they are the recipients of the blessings of the gospel—members of that group of people who have been blessed in Christ by the grace of God.

After the Video

- How does baptism convey the idea of the judgment and curse of God? In what way does baptism symbolize what Jesus did on the cross?

  Baptism is a water ordeal that has roots in the narrative of Old Testament judgment. Paul associates baptism with the baptism of the Israelites in the Red Sea (1 Cor. 10:1–2). Peter draws a parallel between baptism and the baptism of the flood waters. In both the Red Sea and the flood, the enemies of God were destroyed by the water. It was a judgment and curse. Those who were saved in these shadowy baptisms were saved through the waters of judgment. In the same way, we are saved through the judgment that fell on Jesus at the cross.

- What does Paul mean when he says, "The world has been crucified to me"?

  When Paul speaks of the world's being crucified to him, he is not saying that nothing in the world matters in any way whatsoever. Rather, he is saying that the death of Jesus reveals the world to be what it truly is in all its fallenness and vanity. The world will not benefit the believer. If we were to gain the whole world but lose our souls in the process, what would we have gained? The answer to that question—as Jesus and Paul taught—is "nothing." We gain nothing from the world. In contrast, we gain everything on account of Christ crucified.

- How should you respond to the benediction at the end of a worship service?

  In this lesson, Dr. Thomas explained that whenever you hear the benediction proclaimed at the end of the service, you should remember that you are a blessed person—a recipient of the gospel privileges. You should remind yourself that the blessing you are hearing is the good news of the gospel. You can go forward knowing that this is the message in which you stand and by which you are assured of God's blessing.

REVIEW QUIZ

Lesson 14

1. **D.**

   The Jews found the cross to be a symbol of God's abandonment. It was a symbol of the curse of God. Deuteronomy 21:23 says, "A hanged man is cursed by God." The Jews found the cross to be a stumbling block because they couldn't understand why anyone would worship someone who had been crucified.

2. **C.**

   In Galatians 3:13–14, Paul teaches the doctrine of propitiation, namely, that the wrath of God descended on Jesus in our place. He was made a curse for us. Though Jesus is sinless, He received in His body the wages of sin. Jesus substituted Himself for us and took the wrath of God that we deserve. Because Jesus became a curse for us, taking the wrath of God in our place, there is no more wrath for those united to Jesus by faith.

3. **C.**

Since the Judaizers were boasting in their fleshly accomplishments as well as in the number of converts they were leading into their legalistic system, the Apostle Paul declared that his boast was only in the cross. Because Jesus died for him, Paul could say that he was crucified to the world's applause and approval. As he explained in Philippians 3:8, "I have suffered the loss of all things and count them as rubbish, in order that I may gain Christ."

4. **D.**

When God brought Israel through the Red Sea, he separated the waters so that the people could walk through on dry land. When the Egyptians tried to cross, the Lord closed the waters on them—drowning them in the waters of the sea. When Paul spoke of baptism in 1 Corinthians 10, he likened it to the waters of judgment at the Red Sea. While Israel was saved, the Egyptians were drowned under the judgment and curse of God. Baptism is therefore a sign of judgment and curse as well as a sign of salvation.

5. **D.**

Paul was highly educated and extremely intelligent. He was destined to be one of the greatest minds in Judaism. However, after his conversion, the world viewed him as a fool. Paul didn't care about worldly achievement or success. Had Paul remained in Judaism, he would have risen to the top through his accomplishments. However, Paul was committed to going around the world to proclaim Jesus and His crucifixion. He gave his life in service of the gospel. This is why the world viewed him as foolish.

6. **B.**

Throughout church history, Christian churches have ended their worship services with a minister pronouncing a benediction over the congregation. A benediction is a blessing of God. It is not a prayer. It is a reminder of how God has blessed us in Christ. It is a word of God by which we are reminded that we are the recipients and beneficiaries of the gospel. It is a gospel pronouncement of God's blessing on His people, so we are to open our eyes and receive the benediction as a reminder of our standing before God in Christ.